17/2/16
6/5/
2'

Windows 10

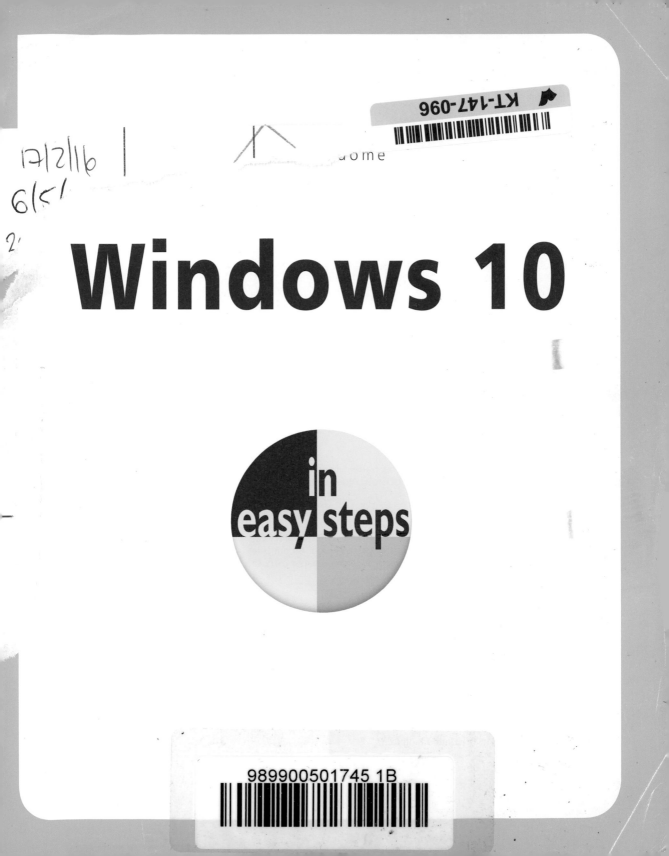

in
easy steps

In easy steps is an imprint of In Easy Steps Limited
16 Hamilton Terrace · Holly Walk · Leamington Spa
Warwickshire · United Kingdom · CV32 4LY
www.ineasysteps.com

Notice of Liability
Every effort has been made to ensure that this book contains accurate
and current information. However, In Easy Steps Limited and the
author shall not be liable for any loss or damage suffered by readers
as a result of any information contained herein.

Trademarks
Microsoft® and Windows® are registered trademarks of Microsoft
Corporation. All other trademarks are acknowledged as belonging to
their respective companies.

In Easy Steps Limited supports The Forest Stewardship Council (FSC),
the leading international forest certification organisation. All our titles
that are printed on Greenpeace approved FSC certified paper carry the
FSC logo.

MIX
Paper from
responsible sources
FSC   FSC® C020837
www.fsc.org

Printed and bound in the United Kingdom

ISBN 978-1-84078-643-9

Contents

1   Introducing Windows 10   7

What is Windows?	8
About Windows 10	9
Windows 10 Interface	10
The Demise of the Charms Bar	12
Obtaining Windows 10	13
Keyboard Shortcuts	14
Windows 10 for Touch	15
Using a Microsoft Account	16
Sign-in Options	18
32-Bit versus 64-Bit	20

2   Getting Started   21

The Start Button	22
The Start Menu	24
Customizing the Start Menu	26
Working with Groups	28
Resizing Tiles	30
The Desktop and Taskbar	32
Shutting Down	33
Task View	34
Adding Desktops	36
Notifications	38
Personalization	40
Lock Screen Settings	42
Settings	44
Searching	56
Setting Up Cortana	58
Using Cortana	59
Setting Reminders	62
Adding and Switching Users	64

3   Working with Apps   67

Starting with Apps	68
Windows 10 Apps	70
Using Windows 10 Apps	72
Classic Apps on the Desktop	74
Closing Apps	75
Viewing All Apps	76
Searching for Apps	77
Pin to Start Menu	78
Pin to Taskbar	79
Using the Windows Store	80
Buying Apps	83
Viewing Your Apps	84
Using Live Tiles	85
Install and Uninstall	86
Task Manager	88
Resource Monitor	90

Basic Controls 91

Menus	92
Dialog Boxes	93
Structure of a Window	94
Moving a Window	95
Restoring a Window	96
Resizing a Window	97
Arranging Windows	98
Snaps	100
Using Multiple Windows	102
Switching Windows	104
Arranging Icons	105
Closing a Window	106

Customizing Windows 107

Using Themes	108
Changing Sound	109
Screen Saver	110
Desktop Icons	111
Screen Resolution	112
Display Settings	113
Ease of Access Center	114
Date and Time Functions	116

File Explorer 117

Opening File Explorer	118
The Taskbar	119
Libraries	120
Scenic Ribbon	121
This PC Folder	123
Quick Access	124
Exploring Drives	126
Address Bar	128
Navigation Panes	130
Changing Views	132
Sorting	133
Filtering	134
Grouping	135
Folder Options	136

Managing Files and Folders 137

Select Files and Folders	138
Copy or Move Files or Folders	140
File Conflicts	144
Open Files	145

Delete Files and Folders 146
The Recycle Bin 147
Create a Folder 150
Rename a File or Folder 151
Backtrack File Operations 152
File Properties 153
Search for Files and Folders 154
Compressed Folders 155
Fonts Folder 157
Character Map 158

8 Digital Lifestyle 159

Using OneDrive 160
Using OneDrive Online 162
OneDrive Settings 163
Adding Files to OneDrive 164
Viewing Photos 166
Editing Photos 170
Groove Music App 174
Playing Music 175
Viewing Movies and TV 177
Playing Games 178

9 Microsoft Edge Browser 179

Internet Connection 180
Introducing the Edge Browser 182
Smart Address Bar 183
Setting a Homepage 184
Using Tabs 185
Bookmarking Web Pages 186
Adding Notes to Web Pages 187
Sharing Notes and Clippings 189
Organizing with the Hub 190
Reading List 192
Reading View 193
Menu Options 194

10 Keeping in Touch 195

Setting Up Mail 196
Working with Mail 198
Finding People 200
Chatting with Skype 204
Using the Calendar 206

11 Networking 209

Network Components 210
Set Up Your Network 211
Internet Connection 212
Discover Networks 214
Network and Sharing Center 215
Join the HomeGroup 216
Sharing Files and Folders 217
Sharing Settings 218
View Network Components 219
Network Troubleshooting 220

12 System and Security 221

System Properties 222
Clean Up Your Disk 224
Windows Update 226
Back Up and Recover Data 227
System Restore 228
Security and Maintenance 230
Windows Firewall 231
Malware Protection 232

Index 233

1 Introducing Windows 10

This chapter explains what Windows is and shows how to get started with the operating system, including the changes in Windows 10 and its interface, keyboard shortcuts, creating a Microsoft Account and signing in.

8 What is Windows?

9 About Windows 10

10 Windows 10 Interface

12 The Demise of the Charms Bar

13 Obtaining Windows 10

14 Keyboard Shortcuts

15 Windows 10 for Touch

16 Using a Microsoft Account

18 Sign-in Options

20 32-Bit versus 64-Bit

What is Windows?

Windows is an operating system for PCs (personal computers). The operating system is the software that organizes and controls all of the components (hardware and software) in your computer so that they integrate and work efficiently together.

The first operating system from Microsoft was known as MS-DOS (Microsoft Disk Operating System). This was a non-graphical, line-oriented, command-driven operating system, able to run only one application at a time.

The original Windows system was an interface manager that ran on top of the MS-DOS system, providing a graphical user interface and using clever processor and memory management to allow it to run more than one application or function at a time.

The basic element of Windows was its 'windowing' capability. A window (with a lower-case w) is a rectangular area used to display information or to run a program. Several windows can be opened at the same time so that you can work with multiple applications. This provided a dramatic increase in productivity, in comparison with the original MS-DOS.

Microsoft released four versions of this interface management Windows, with numerous intermediate versions, including:

- 1985 – Windows 1.0; 1987 – Windows 2.0, 2.1 and 2.11; 1990 – Windows 3.0, 3.1, 3.11 (Windows for Workgroups); 1995 – Windows 95; 1998 – Windows 98, 98 SE; 2000 – Windows Me (Millennium Edition).

The next version, Windows XP, was a full operating system in its own right. This was eventually followed by Windows Vista and then Windows 7, 8 and 8.1.

- 2001 – Windows XP (eXPerience) Home and Professional.

- 2007 – Windows Vista Home, Home Premium, Ultimate etc.

- 2009 – Windows 7 Starter, Home Premium, Ultimate etc.

- 2012 – Windows 8 Starter, Pro, Enterprise and RT.

- 2013 – Windows 8.1 Starter, Pro, Enterprise and RT.

The New icon pictured above indicates a new or enhanced feature introduced with Windows 10.

8

About Windows 10

The latest version of Windows was released in July 2015:

- 2015 – Windows 10 Home, Pro, Enterprise and Education

All major computer operating systems (OS) undergo regular upgrades and new versions. Sometimes these are a significant visual overhaul, while others concentrate more on the behind-the-scenes aspect of the OS. In the terms of Windows, Windows 8 was one of the most radical updates to the User Interface (UI) and introduced a number of new features, for both desktop and mobile versions of Windows. However, it was not met with universal approval, as it was perceived that it was two separate operating systems (desktop and mobile) bolted together and not satisfying each environment completely.

With Windows 10 a lot of the problems with Windows 8 have been addressed: the familiar Start Menu has been reinstated to return to a similar UI to earlier versions of Windows; there has been greater consolidation between desktop and mobile devices running Windows 10; and the operation of apps has been standardized so that it is similar for the new Windows apps and also the more traditional ones. In a sense, this is a case of going back one step in order to go forwards two steps and Windows 10 has succeeded in creating a familiar environment, coupled with a range of new features.

New features

Added to this are a number of new features, including a new web browser, Microsoft Edge, that allows users to draw on and annotate web pages and then send them to other people.

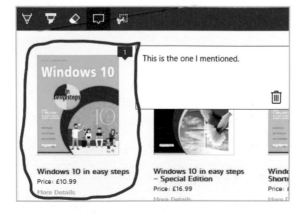

This is the one I mentioned.

Windows 10 in easy steps
Price: £10.99
More Details

Windows 10 in easy steps – Special Edition
Price: £16.99
More Details

Wind
Short
Price:
More D

There is also a new Personal Digital Assistant voice function, Cortana, to help elevate Windows 10 to be the most advanced operating system that Microsoft has produced.

Don't forget

Windows 10 is a free upgrade for users of most versions of Windows 7, 8 or 8.1 (excluding Enterprise).

Don't forget

If you are upgrading from Windows 7, 8 or 8.1 you will be able to keep all of your settings, files and apps.

Windows 10 Interface

Windows 8 was one of the most significant changes to the Windows operating system since Windows 95 helped redefine the way that we look at personal computers. It aimed to bring

the desktop and mobile computing environments together, principally with the brightly colored Start screen and Charms bar. However, this proved to be awkward for a lot of users, with Windows 8 not fully meeting the needs of the device they were using.

The Windows 10 interface has been redesigned so that it looks as similar as possible, regardless of whether it is being used on a desktop computer with a mouse and keyboard, or on a mobile or touchscreen device (and most of the underlying functionality is still the same).

Windows 10 will look more familiar to users of pre-Windows 8 versions of Windows. It opens at the Desktop, where shortcuts to items can be placed, and the Taskbar is at the bottom of the screen. The Start screen format and the Charms bar have also been replaced with more traditional elements of the Windows operating system, including the reinstated Start Menu.

Don't forget

The main recommended specifications for PCs and laptops running Windows 10 are: 1GHz processor; 1GB RAM (32-bit Windows) or 2GB RAM (64-bit Windows); and 16GB of free disk space for installation.

Start Menu

The Start Menu has been reinstated in Windows 10. This will be more familiar to pre-Windows 8 users, although it has been redesigned so that it also includes a range of colored tiles, which can be pinned to the Start Menu and are used to access the most commonly used apps. The left-hand side of the Start Menu contains links to some of your most frequently used functions (such as the Power button) and most used apps.

The Settings app can be used to customize the Start Menu (**Settings > Personalization > Start**).

Windows 10 for Touchscreen

The Windows 10 version that is optimized for touchscreen use is designed for using with a tablet (such as the Microsoft Surface 3) where all

of the screen navigation can be done by tapping, swiping and pinching on the screen. These features can also be used on touchscreen desktops and laptops that have this functionality (see page 15 for details).

The Demise of the Charms Bar

One of the features in Windows 8 and 8.1 that did not meet with universal approval was the Charms bar. This was a bar of icons that appeared at the right-hand side of the screen when the cursor was moved to certain positions. The Charms bar consisted of: a Settings Charm, which was used for quick settings, including the Power button, and the full PC Settings; a Device Charm for adding external devices; a Sharing Charm; and a Search Charm.

In Windows 10 the Charms Bar has been removed and its functionality has been incorporated into other features:

In Windows 8 and 8.1 the PC Settings were accessed from the Charms bar. The Settings in Windows 10 can be accessed from a range of locations, including the Start Menu and the Notification panel. See page 44 for details.

- **Power button**. This is now available on the Start Menu, which is accessed from the Start Button in the bottom left-hand corner of the screen.

- **Notifications** and **Quick access settings**. These are now available from the Notifications button at the right-hand side of the Taskbar at the bottom of the Desktop. (This is also known as the Action Center).

- **Search**. This is now incorporated into the Taskbar, to the right of the Start Button. It also includes the new Cortana search function which is accessed from the microphone icon.

- **Device** and **Sharing** options. These are now incorporated into the menu within some of the modern Windows 10 apps. Click on the menu to access the options.

Obtaining Windows 10

Windows 10 is a slight departure by Microsoft in that it is being promoted as an online service, rather than just a standalone operating system. This means that, by default, Windows 10 is obtained and downloaded online, with subsequent updates and upgrades provided on a regular basis.

The three main options for obtaining Windows 10 are:

- **Upgrade** – Replace an older version of Windows, retaining the installed applications and settings. This can only be done with Windows 7 and later: for earlier versions you will need to install a new, full copy of Windows 10. **If you already have Windows 7, 8 or 8.1 it is free to upgrade to Windows 10**.

- **Clean Install** – This has to be done if you have Windows XP or Windows Vista and you want to upgrade to Windows 10. (See the Don't Forget tip).

- **Pre-install** – Buy a new PC or laptop with Windows 10 already installed, then install the required apps.

For users of Windows 7, 8, or 8.1, Windows 10 is a free upgrade (as long as you upgrade within a year of its release on 29 July 2015). Ensure Windows Update is turned on within Settings to ensure you are informed about the upgrade. When it is available you will be notified and you will be able to download and install the free upgrade (this should all be done automatically). Once it has been installed you will receive upgrades and updates as they become available. (In some cases, there may be a Get Windows 10 app located at the right-hand side of the Taskbar that can be used to obtain the upgrade to Windows 10).

Some of the steps that the installation will go through are:

- **Personalize**. These are settings that will be applied to your version of Windows 10. They include the color for the Start Menu, a name for your computer and a connection to a wireless network. These settings can be selected within the Settings app once Windows 10 has been installed too.

- **Settings**. You can choose to have express settings applied, or customize them.

- **Microsoft Account**. You can set up a Microsoft Account during installation, or once you have started Windows 10.

Windows 7 Enterprise and Windows 8/8.1 Enterprise are excluded from the free upgrade.

If you have a version of Windows that is earlier than Windows 7 (e.g. Vista or XP) you will have to pay for the upgrade to Windows 10. This will be with a DVD and costs US$119 (£99). This requires a clean install which means that your files and settings will be removed. It is essential that these are backed up before the installation is started.

You may need your license number for the free upgrade from Windows 7, 8 or 8.1 so make sure you have this.

Keyboard Shortcuts

As you become more confident using Windows 10 you may want to access certain items more quickly. There is a range of keyboard shortcuts that can be used to access some of the items you use most frequently.

The majority of the shortcuts are accessed together with the WinKey. To use the keyboard shortcuts press:

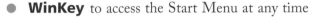

- **WinKey** to access the Start Menu at any time

- **WinKey** + **L** to lock the computer and display the Lock screen

- **WinKey** + **I** to access the Settings app

- **WinKey** + **K** to connect new devices

- **WinKey** + **H** to access the Sharing options for the current items or app

- **WinKey** + **Q** to access the Personal Digital Assistant voice function, Cortana

- **WinKey** + **D** to access the Desktop

- **WinKey** + **M** to access the Desktop with the active window minimized

- **WinKey** + **E** to access File Explorer, displaying the Quick Access section

- **WinKey** + **T** to display the thumbnails on the Desktop Taskbar

- **WinKey** + **U** to access the Ease of Access Center

- **WinKey** + **X** to access administration tools and quick access to items including the Desktop and the Control Panel

- **Alt** + **F4** to close a Windows 10 app

- **Ctrl** + **Shift** + **Esc** to access the Task Manager

Windows 10 for Touch

One of the aims of Windows 10 is to make the operating system more familiar again to users with a keyboard and mouse. This has been done by reverting back to a more traditional look and feel than that of Windows 8 and 8.1. For touchscreen devices, such as tablets, laptops with precision touchpads and phones, the same overall operation of Windows 10 has been maintained so that users can feel comfortable with the operating system regardless of the device on which they are using it.

Continuum

Continuum refers to the function of Windows 10 where you can start something on one Windows 10 device and then continue working on it on another. For instance, you could start a letter in Word on a desktop computer, save it, and pick up where you left off on the Microsoft tablet, Surface 3. Continuum works between desktop computers, laptops, tablets and Windows phones.

Using touch

Touchscreen devices and those with precision touchpads can be used with Windows 10 to navigate through a number of gestures, swipes and taps on the screen or touchpad. The range of these gestures has been consolidated from Windows 8 and 8.1, since these included a number of options for accessing the Charms that are no longer available with Windows 10. Some of the gestures that can be used with touchscreen or touchpad devices using Windows 10 are:

- Swipe inwards from the right-hand edge to access the Action Center (Notification Center).

- Swipe inwards from the left-hand edge to access the Task View for currently open apps.

- In an open Windows 10 app, swipe downwards from the top of the screen to access the app's toolbar.

- In an open Windows 10 app, use a long swipe downwards from the top of the screen to close the app.

- Swipe upwards from the bottom of the screen to access the Taskbar (when an app is at full screen).

- Tap with three fingers on a touchpad to bring up the Personal Digital Assistant, Cortana.

Hot tip

Aside from the gestures used on a touchscreen device, much of the operation of Windows 10 has been consolidated between computers with a mouse and keyboard, and mobile devices.

Using a Microsoft Account

We live in a world of ever-increasing computer connectivity, where users expect to be able to access their content wherever they are and share it with their friends and family in a variety of ways, whether it is by email, messaging or photo sharing. This is known as cloud computing, with content being stored on online servers, from where it can be accessed by authorized users.

In Windows 10 this type of connectivity is achieved with a Microsoft Account. This is a registration system (which can be set up with most email addresses and a password) that provides access to a number of services via the Windows 10 apps. These include:

- **Mail**. This is the Windows 10 email app that can be used to access and manage your different email accounts.

- **Skype**. This is the text messaging and video chatting app.

- **People**. This is the address book app.

- **Calendar**. This is the calendar and organizer app.

- **The Windows Store**. This is the online store for previewing and downloading additional apps.

- **OneDrive**. This is the online backup and sharing service.

Creating a Microsoft Account

It is free to create a Microsoft Account and can be done with an email address and, together with a password, this provides a unique identifier for logging into your Microsoft Account and the related apps. There are several ways in which you can create and set up a Microsoft Account:

- During the initial setup process when you install Windows 10. You will be asked if you want to create a Microsoft Account at this point. If you do not, you can always do so at a later time.

- When you first open an app that requires access to a Microsoft Account. When you do this you will be prompted to create a new account.

- From the **Accounts** section of the **Settings** app (for more information about the Settings app see pages 44-55).

Beware

Without a Microsoft Account you will not be able to access the full functionality of the apps listed here.

Whichever way you use to create a Microsoft Account the process
is similar:

1 When you are first
prompted to sign
in with a Microsoft
Account you can
enter your account
details, if you have
one, or

> ### Add your Microsoft account
> Sign in with your Microsoft account. You can use this account with other apps
> on this device. Learn more.
>
> someone@example.com
>
> Password
>
> Forgot my password
>
> No account? Create one!

2 Click on the **No account?
Create one!** link

> No account? Create one!

3 Enter your name, an
email address and a
password for your
Microsoft Account

> ### Let's create your account
> Windows, Office, Outlook.com, OneDrive, Skype, Xbox. They're all better and
> more personal when you sign in with your Microsoft account.* Learn more
>
> Nick   Vandome
>
> ✓ After you sign up, we'll send you a message with a link
> to verify this user name.
>
> nickvandome2@gmail.com
> Get a new email address
>
> ••••••••
>
> United States   ⌄
>
> Birth month ⌄ Day ⌄ Year ⌄
>
> Back   Next

Hot tip

Microsoft Account
details can also be used
as your sign-in
for Windows 10 (see
pages 18-19).

17

4 Click on the **Next** button to move
through the registration process

> Next

5 Enter your password
again to confirm your
account

6 Click on the **Finish**
button in the final
window to complete
setting up your
Microsoft Account

> ### Make it yours
> Windows is better when your settings and files automatically sync. If you make
> nickvandome2@gmail.com your primary account, Windows will use it
> automatically with your Microsoft services, and for signing in to your device.
>
> To make nickvandome2@gmail.com your primary account, we'll need your
> Windows password one last time to make sure it's really you.
>
> Your Windows password
>
> I'll connect my Microsoft account later.
>
> Next

Sign-in Options

Each time you start up your computer you will need to sign in. This is a security feature so that no-one can gain unauthorized access to your account on your PC. This sign-in process starts with the Lock screen and then you have to enter your sign-in password.

1 When you start your PC the Lock screen will be showing. This is linked to the sign-in screen

2 Click on the **Lock screen**, or press any key, to move to the sign-in screen. Enter your password and press **Enter** or click on this arrow

3 On the sign-in screen, click on this button to select Ease of Access options

4 Click on this button to select Power off options including Shut Down and Restart

For details about personalizing the Lock screen see pages 42-43.

You can lock your PC at any point by pressing the **WinKey** + **L**.

You will get an error message if you enter the wrong password or if you simply mis-key and cause an incorrect character to be added.

5 If there are other users with an account on the same PC, their names will be displayed here

6 Click on another user to access their own sign-in screen

Sign-in settings

Settings for how you sign in can be accessed from the Users section in the Settings app:

1 Access the **Settings** app and click on the **Accounts** button

Accounts
Your account, sync settings, work, other users

2 Under **Sign-in options**, select options to change your password, create a picture password or create a PIN instead of a password

3 If you want to create a picture password you must have a touchscreen device. Select a picture and draw a pattern to use as your sign-in

Don't forget

You can sign in with a Local account or a Microsoft Account. If you sign in with the latter you will have access to the related services, such as Mail and People. Also, you will be able to sync your settings and use them on another computer with your Account.

Don't forget

For details about using the Settings app see pages 44-55.

Hot tip

Windows Hello is a function that uses biometric authentication for signing in to Windows 10. This is either done by scanning your face or with a fingerprint reader. However, specialist hardware is required and this is not available on many devices at present.

19

32-Bit versus 64-Bit

As well as choosing your Windows 10 edition, you also need to decide between the 32-bit and the 64-bit versions of the operating system. This choice is available for all editions of Windows 10, including installation DVDs for each mode.

The 32-bit or 64-bit nomenclature refers to the memory address length which the processor can reference. This dictates the maximum amount of memory, which is 4GB for 32-bit mode (or more accurately 3.4GB, since some memory needs to be allocated for other purposes). For 64-bit mode, the maximum may be much higher, though the Windows 10 editions do not make full use of the potential. As well as more memory, 64-bit mode will also be faster; typically about 10%.

However, you need applications that are specifically optimized for 64-bit processing to take advantage of the speed improvements and memory increase. Many games, for example, include the necessary enhancements.

Remember that choosing a 64-bit system means that you can no longer run 16-bit applications. This is only a problem if you use very old software (from the Windows 3.1 days).

More importantly, existing 32-bit drivers for your devices will not operate in 64-bit mode, so you will have to locate 64-bit versions of the drivers. You may have problems with some devices, particularly the older ones.

You may also find that running 32-bit applications in a 64-bit operating system might actually be slower, due to the additional overheads imposed by conversion between the address systems.

In summary, if you have a 64-bit capable computer but use older hardware or 32-bit applications, you might do better to stay with the 32-bit version of Windows 10. With the latest hardware and drivers, and applications that are 64-bit optimized, for especially demanding applications such as video editing or image packages, the switch to 64-bit and higher memory would offer significant improvements.

It will not be long before 64-bit computing becomes the standard, and 32-bit operation becomes an optional extra, but for the present there are still large numbers of 32-bit applications.

To check whether your version of Windows 10 is 32-bit or 64-bit, right-click on the Start Button and click on the **System** link. The bit version is displayed under the **System > System type** section.

2 Getting Started

Windows 10 improves upon the radical design of Windows 8 and returns to a lot of the more traditional elements of Windows, such as the return of the Start Menu. This chapter looks at some of the main features of Windows 10, focusing on the redesigned Start Menu and using the Desktop and the Taskbar. It also covers the personal assistant, Cortana, for voice searching over your computer and setting reminders for a range of items.

22 The Start Button

24 The Start Menu

26 Customizing the Start Menu

28 Working with Groups

30 Resizing Tiles

32 The Desktop and Taskbar

33 Shutting Down

34 Task View

36 Adding Desktops

38 Notifications

40 Personalization

42 Lock Screen Settings

44 Settings

56 Searching

58 Setting Up Cortana

59 Using Cortana

62 Setting Reminders

64 Adding and Switching Users

The Start Button

When the predecessor to Windows 10 (Windows 8) was introduced there was a significant outcry due to the disappearance of the traditional Windows Start Button. This was made worse by the removal of the Start Menu too. However, the Start Button was reinstated in Windows 8.1 and the Start Menu has now also returned, in an enhanced format. This means that Windows 10 can be used in a similar way to traditional versions of Windows.

Using the Start Button

The Start Button provides access to the apps on your Windows 10 PC and also to the enhanced Start Menu:

 Click on the **Start Button** in the bottom left-hand corner of the screen

 The **Start Menu** is displayed

3 The left-hand side of the Start Menu contains links to frequently used apps and a list of quick links to items such as the Power button and All apps (these can be customized within the **Personalization > Start** section of the Settings app)

Click on the **Power** button on the Start Menu to access options for Sleep, Shutting Down or Restart.

 The right-hand side of the Start Menu is where apps can be pinned so that they are always available. This is displayed as a collection of large, colored, tiles

 Other items can also be accessed from the Start Button by right-clicking on it

Start Button functionality

Although the Start Button is different to earlier versions of
Windows, it still has a range of functionality:

 Right-click on the
Start Button to view
its menu

Programs and Features
Mobility Center
Power Options
Event Viewer
System
Device Manager
Network Connections
Disk Management
Computer Management
Command Prompt
Command Prompt (Admin)
Task Manager
Control Panel
File Explorer
Search
Run
Shut down or sign out   >
Desktop

The Start Button menu
in Step 1 has a number
of options for accessing
system functions, such
as Command Prompt
and Disk Management.

② Click on the relevant
buttons to view items
including the **Desktop**
and **Control Panel**

Control Panel
File Explorer
Search
Run
Shut down or sign out   >
Desktop
Search the web and Windows

23

③ Shut down options are also available from the
Start Button (see page 33)

The Start Menu

The reinstated Start Menu in Windows 10 is where you can access areas within your computer, perform certain functions and also access apps from a variety of locations. Some of the default items on the Start Menu can be customized to a certain extent (see pages 26-27) and there is considerable functionality here:

 Click here to access your own account settings or sign out from your account

 Your most frequently used apps are displayed here. Click on one to open it (these items will change as you use different apps)

Nick Vandome

Most used

Snagit 11 Editor

Notepad

Alarms & Clock

Scan

Reading List

WordPad

Store

Recently added

Microsoft Solitaire Collection

File Explorer

Settings

Power

All apps

Search the web and Wi

 Click here to access items including the **File Explorer**, your **Documents** library within File Explorer and the Windows 10 **Settings**

 Click on the **Power** button for options to **Sleep** your computer, **Shut Down** or **Restart**

File

Sleep

Shut down

Setti

Restart

Power

5 Click on the **All apps** button to access a list of all of the apps on your computer. Use the scroll bar at the right-hand side to move through the list of apps

Click on a letter at the top of a section of apps to view an alphabetic grid. Click on a letter to move to that section.

25

6 Click on the **Back** button return to the standard Start Menu view

7 If there is a down-pointing arrow next to an app this means that there are additional items that can be accessed. Click on the arrow to view these

Full screen mode is designed more for tablets, and if you use it the Start Menu will occupy the whole screen.

Customizing the Start Menu

Windows 10 is very adaptable and can be customized in several ways, so that it works the best for you. This includes the Start Menu which can be set to behave in certain ways and have specific items added to it. To do this:

1 Open the **Settings** app and click on the **Personalization** button

2 Click on the **Start** button

3 Under **Start**, select whether to show most used apps or recently used apps on the Start Menu, show the Start Menu full screen, or display recently opened items in Jump List format

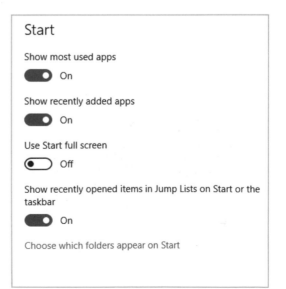

4 Click on the **Choose which folders appear on Start** button to select the items that appear on the Start Menu

Choose which folders appear on Start

5 Drag the buttons **On** or **Off** for the items you want to appear on the Start Menu, i.e. the File Explorer, the Settings app and the Music app

Don't forget

If you find that you do not use some items very much once they have been added to the Start Menu, they can be removed by dragging their buttons to **Off** in Step 5.

6 The items selected in Step 5 appear on the Start Menu, above the Power button

Working with Groups

By default, the apps on the Start Menu are arranged in groups, such as Everyday apps. However, apps can be arranged into other groups, and new ones can also be created, by dragging apps between groups. To do this:

 Click and hold on a tile and drag it away from its current group, into a space in a new group. If there is no space the other apps will move to accommodate the new one

 Drag the tile into its new position to create a new group

 Click and drag on the title bar of a group to move the whole group

...cont'd

Naming Groups
In their initial state, groups on the Start Menu are either not named, or they have a default name, but it is possible to give them all their own individual names or titles. To do this:

1 Move the cursor over the top of a group and click on the current name or on this button at the right-hand side

Everyday apps ═

2 Double-click on the current name

Everyday apps

3 Enter a name for the group

My best apps

4 The name is applied at the top of the group

Group names can be edited with the same process as when creating them in the first place.

Resizing Tiles

As well as rearranging tiles, their sizes can also be edited on the Start Menu. Depending on the Windows app, there may be up to four options for resizing tiles in Windows 10: wide, large, medium and small, with the initial selection made for you:

 Right-click on a tile to select it and click on the **Resize** button

 The current size of the tile is shown with a tick next to it

 Click on another option to resize the tile

 If the size is smaller, the tile is reduced in size and a gap appears next to it

(unless there is another tile small enough to fill the space next to it)

5 For a wide tile, there will be options for making it **Large**, **Medium** or **Small**

6 The **Large** size is the biggest available option for resizing tiles. Tiles that have been resized can be moved around the Start Menu and other tiles will move automatically to accommodate them

Hot tip

The **Large** size is a good option for a tile that can then be used as a live tile to display its contents or real-time information.

7 Creating a range of different tile sizes is a good way to organize the Start Menu and create a good mixture from a design point of view

The Desktop and Taskbar

After the use of the Start Screen in Windows 8 and 8.1, the Desktop is once again an integral part of Windows, and when you boot up Windows 10 it opens at the Desktop. This also displays the Taskbar, at the bottom of the screen:

Shortcut icons   Search box   Desktop background

Start Button   Task View button   Taskbar

1   Move the cursor over items on the Taskbar to see open windows for that item. Click on a window to make that the active one

2   The Notifications area at the right-hand side of the Taskbar has speaker, network and other system tools. Click on one to see more information about that item

Shutting Down

The method of shutting down in Windows 8 was another contentious issue and one which has been addressed in Windows 10 by adding this functionality to the Start Menu.

Shutting down from the Start Menu

 Click on the **Start Button**

 Click on the **Power** button

 Click on either the **Sleep, Shut down** or **Restart** buttons; or

 Right-click on the **Start Button** and select either **Sign out, Sleep**, **Shut down** or **Restart**

File Explorer		Sign out
Search		Sleep
Run		Shut down
Shut down or sign out	>	Restart
Desktop		

Search the web and Windows

For some updates to Windows you will need to restart your computer for them to take effect.

33

Task View

A new feature in Windows 10 is the Task View option. This is located on the Taskbar and can be used to view all open apps and also add new desktops. To use Task View:

1 Click on this button on the Taskbar

2 To show or hide the Task View button, right-click on the button and check On or Off the **Show Task View button** option

Toolbars	>
Search	>
✓ Show Task View button	
Show Touch Keyboard button	

3 The Task View displays minimized versions of the currently open apps and windows

Apps can only be open on one desktop at a time. So if an app is open on one desktop and you try to open it on another, you will be taken to the desktop with the already open app. For adding additional desktops, see pages 36-37.

34

4 As more windows are opened the format is arranged accordingly

5 If an app has more than one window open, e.g. File Explorer, each window is displayed within Task View

Don't forget

Although the shortcuts and background are the same for each Desktop, the Taskbar will change depending on the open apps.

6 Click on a window in Task View to make it the active window

Adding Desktops

Another function within Task View is for creating additional desktops. This can be useful if you want to separate different categories of tasks on your computer. For instance, you may want to keep your open entertainment apps on a different desktop from your productivity ones. To create additional desktops:

1 Click on the **Task View** button on the Taskbar

2 The current desktop is displayed with the open windows

If you add too many desktops it may become confusing in terms of the content on each one.

3 Click on the **New desktop** button

4 The new desktop is displayed at the bottom of the Task View window

5 Click on the new desktop to access it. Each desktop has the same background and shortcuts

The default names of different desktops cannot be changed, i.e. they are Desktop 1, Desktop 2, etc.

37

6 Open apps on the new desktop. These will be separate from the apps on any other desktop

To delete a desktop, click on the Task View button and click on the cross next to the desktop you want to remove.

7 Click on the **Task View** button to move between desktops

Notifications

In the modern digital world there is an increasing desire to keep updated about what is happening in our online world. With Windows 10, the Notifications panel (Action Center) can be used to display information from a variety of sources, so that you never miss an update or a notification from one of your apps. To view your notifications:

1 Click on the **Notifications** button on the Taskbar

2 New notifications appear at the top of the panel (for selecting what appears, see next page)

Click on a notification to open it and view its full contents.

ACTION CENTER   Clear all

Security and Maintenance

⚠   Verify your identity on this PC   Thu
    Your saved credentials for apps, websites   ⌄

Settings

⚙   Updates were installed   3:28p

Collapse ⌄

Tablet mode	Connect	Note	All settings
Battery saver	VPN	Bluetooth	100%
PlusnetWireless s792287	Quiet hours	Location	Airplane mode

Ph... ^ 🔊 ◀× 📶 📡 💬 ENG   12:08 PM 7/19/2015

Notifications for certain apps also appear onscreen for a short period of time in a small banner, to alert you to the fact that there is a new notification.

3 Quick action buttons appear at the bottom of the panel. Click on an item to activate or deactivate it (when a button is blue the item is active)

Settings for Notifications

To apply settings for the Notifications panel:

1 Click on the **Settings** app and access **System > Notifications & actions**

2 Under the **Quick action** heading, click on the **Select which icons appear on the taskbar** link to select items for the Taskbar

3 Click on the **Turn system icons on or off** link to turn **On** or **Off** the default items on the Taskbar

4 Under the **Show notifications from these apps** heading, drag the buttons **On** or **Off** to specify the items that appear in the Notifications

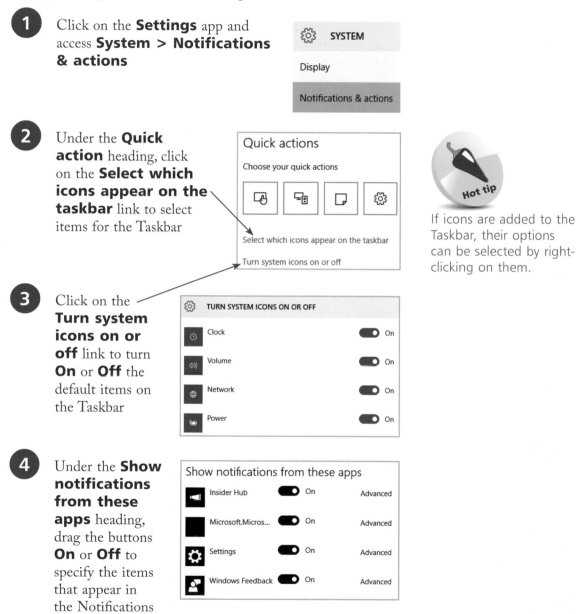

Hot tip

If icons are added to the Taskbar, their options can be selected by right-clicking on them.

panel. For instance, if the **Email and accounts** button (or the **Mail** button) is **On**, you will be notified whenever you receive a new email

Personalization

Chapter 5 details a range of personalization options that can be applied from the Control Panel. Within the Personalization section of the Settings app there are also options to personalize the look of Windows 10. To do this:

 Open the **Settings** app and click on the **Personalization** button

Personalization
Background, lock screen, colors

In Windows 10 more of the personalization options have been moved into the Settings app. However, there are still some options within the Control panel, including themes, sounds and the screen saver. See Chapter 5 for details.

 Click on the **Background** button to select a Desktop background. Select **Picture** in the Background box and click to select a picture or click on the **Browse** button to select one of your own pictures

 Click on the **Colors** button to select an accent color for the current background, Start Menu and Taskbar

4 Drag this button to **Off** to disable the automatic selection for the accent color

5 Click on one of the colors to select it for the accent color

6 Drag this button **On** to use the color selected in Step 5 on the Start Menu, Taskbar and Action Center

7 Drag this button **On** to make the Start Menu, Taskbar and Action Center transparent

8 Click on the **Themes** button to select a color theme for Windows 10. Some of these will be available from the **Classic theme settings** button which links to themes used in previous versions of Windows

Hot tip

For details about personalizing the Lock screen, see pages 42-43.

41

Lock Screen Settings

The Settings app enables you to set the appearance of the Lock screen, the Start Menu and select an account photo. To do this, first access the Settings:

1 Open the **Settings** app and click on the **Personalization** button

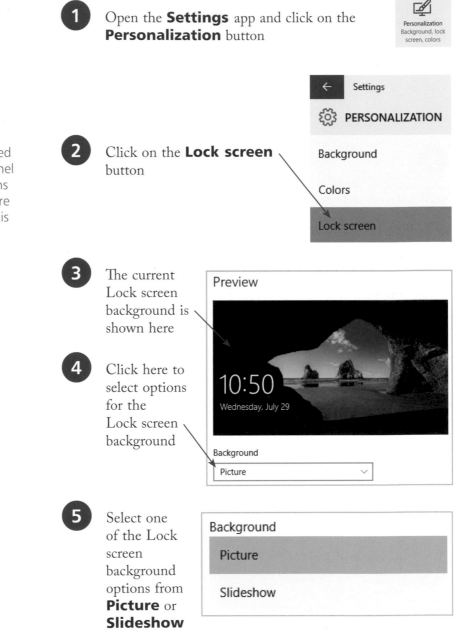

2 Click on the **Lock screen** button

3 The current Lock screen background is shown here

4 Click here to select options for the Lock screen background

5 Select one of the Lock screen background options from **Picture** or **Slideshow**

6 For the Picture option, click on the **Browse** button to select your own picture

Notifications can be set to appear on the Lock screen. Do this under the Lock screen heading in the Personalize section of the Settings app.

7 Select an image and click on **Choose picture** to add this to the background options for the Lock screen

DSC_0815	DSC_0816
All files	
Choose picture	Cancel

8 Other options for the Lock screen include selecting apps that display their detailed or quick status, options for screen timeout when not in use and screen saver settings

If you use your own images for the Lock screen background, these will remain available on the thumbnail row even if you switch to another image for the background.

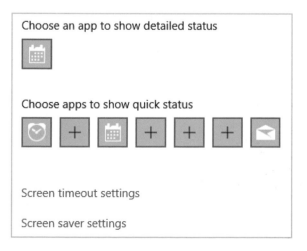

Choose an app to show detailed status

Choose apps to show quick status

Screen timeout settings

Screen saver settings

Settings

Accessing Settings

The Settings in Windows 10 provide options for how you set up your computer and how it operates. There are nine main categories of Settings, each of which have a number of sub-categories. The Settings app can be accessed in a number of ways:

1 Click on the **Start button**

2 Click on the **Settings** button on the Start Menu or the **Settings** tile on the Start Menu; or

3 Click on the **Notifications** button on the Taskbar

4 Click on the **All settings** button; or

5 Enter **Settings** into the **Search** box and click on the **Settings** button

6 In the **Settings** app, click on one of the main categories to view the options within that category

Hot tip

Add the Settings app to the Taskbar for quick access. To do this, access it from the Start Menu, right-click on it and click on **Pin to taskbar**.

System Settings

The System Settings provide numerous options to specify how your computer looks and operates. They include:

- **Display**. This contains options for changing the size of items on the screen, the orientation of the screen and options for adjusting the screen brightness, either manually or automatically.

- **Notifications & actions**. This contains options for selecting which notification icons appear on the Taskbar and specifying which apps can be used to display notifications, e.g. your calendar and email.

- **Apps & features**. This contains information about the apps that you have on your computer. This includes their size and installation date. Click on an app and click on the **Uninstall** button to remove it.

Apps can also be uninstalled from within the Control Panel (**Programs > Uninstall a program**).

Settings — □ ×

⚙ SYSTEM — Find a setting 🔍

Display
Notifications & actions
Apps & features
Multitasking
Tablet mode
Battery saver
Power & sleep
Storage
Offline maps

Apps & features

Manage optional features

Search, sort, and filter by drive. If you would like to uninstall or move an app, select it from the list.

Type an app name... 🔍

Sort by size ∨

Show apps on all drives ∨

Adobe Creative Suite 5 Design Premium   3.51 GB
Adobe Systems Incorporated   7/13/2015

Adobe Photoshop Elements 13   3.43 GB
Adobe Systems Incorporated   7/13/2015

- **Multitasking**. This contains options for working with windows and desktops. In the **Snap** section you can turn on options for arranging windows when they are moved to the edge of the screen, and in the **Virtual desktops** sections you can specify whether the Taskbar (and Alt + Tab) shows all open windows, or just those for the current desktop.

- **Tablet mode**. This can be used on desktop and laptop computers using a mouse and keyboard to replicate the operation of using a touchscreen device or tablet with Windows 10. This includes expanding the Start Menu to full screen.

...cont'd

- **Battery saver**. This can be used on laptops and displays the charge level of the battery and what is using the battery most. It also has options for saving battery power.

- **Power & sleep**. This contains options for when the screen is turned off when not being used and when the computer goes to sleep when it is not being used. This ranges from one minute to never.

- **Storage**. This displays how much storage has been taken up on your computer and has options for where you want to save certain types of content. This can be the PC or an external drive.

- **Offline maps**. This contains options for downloading maps so that you can use them even when you are offline. There is also an option for only downloading maps when you are connected to Wi-Fi, to save any unwanted charges if you have a mobile data plan.

- **Default apps**. This contains options for selecting default apps that open for specific tasks, such as for web browsing, playing music or viewing photos.

- **About.** This contains information about your computer and the version of Windows that you are using.

Devices Settings

The Devices Settings provide settings for how the hardware connected with your computer operates. They include:

- **Printers & scanners**. This can be used to add new printers or scanners to your computer. These can either be wireless ones, or ones which connect via cable. In most cases, the required software will be installed with Windows 10 or, if not, it will be downloaded from the internet.

- **Connected devices**. This can be used to add new devices, such as a printer, using the **Add a device** button.

- **Bluetooth**. This can be used to link your computer to compatible Bluetooth devices, so that they can share content over short distances with radiowaves. The two devices have to be 'paired' initially to be able to share content.

- **Mouse & touchpad**. This contains options for customizing the mouse and touchpad (for a laptop). These include setting the main button on the mouse (Left by default) and how the scrolling operates with the mouse, such as the number of lines that can be scrolled at a time (Multiple by default).

Printers can also be added through the **Control Panel**. This is done in the **Hardware and Sound** section, under **Devices and Printers**. Click on the **Add a printer** button and follow the wizard.

47

- **Typing**. This contains options for correcting your typing as you go. These include autocorrecting misspelt words and highlighting misspelt words.

- **AutoPlay**. This contains options for applying AutoPlay for external devices such as removable drives and memory cards. If AutoPlay is On, the devices will be activated and accessed when they are attached to your computer.

...cont'd

Network & Internet Settings

The Network & Internet Settings provide settings related to connecting to networks, usually for accessing the internet. They include:

- **Wi-Fi**. This contains options for connecting to the internet via your Wi-Fi router (or a public hotspots if you are away from home). There is also an option for managing your Wi-Fi networks.

If Wi-Fi is turned **On** in the Wi-Fi settings, any routers in range should be recognized. A password will probably then be required to connect to the router.

← Settings		– □ ×
⚙ NETWORK & INTERNET		Find a setting

Wi-Fi

Airplane mode

Data usage

VPN

Dial-up

Ethernet

Wi-Fi

On

PlusnetWireless792287
Connected

virginmedia6249958

CRG

- **Airplane mode**. This can be used to turn off wireless communication when you are on a plane, so that you can still use your computer (laptop) safely.

- **Data usage**. This displays how much data has been downloaded over any networks that you are using. The most common one is Wi-Fi and displays your usage over a 30 day period.

- **VPN**. This can be used to connect to a corporate network over VPN (Virtual Private Network). If you are doing this you will need certain settings from your network administrator.

- **Dial-up**. This can be used if you have a dial-up modem for connecting to the internet. This is not common these days but is still a valid means of internet access.

- **Ethernet**. This can be used if you are connecting to the internet with an Ethernet cable. This connects to the Ethernet port on your computer and internet access is delivered through using your telephone line.

- **Proxy**. This contains options for using a proxy server for Ethernet or Wi-Fi connections.

Personalization Settings

The Personalization Settings provide options for customizing the look and feel of Windows 10. They include:

● **Background**. This can be used to change the Desktop background in Windows 10. You can select images from the pictures provided, solid colors, a slideshow or your own photos (using the **Browse** button). You can also choose how the background fits the screen (the default is for Fill).

● **Colors**. This contains options for selecting a color for borders, buttons, the Taskbar and the Start Menu background.

● **Lock screen**. This can be used to select a background for the Lock screen. You can use the images provided and also select your own photos (using the **Browse** button). You can also select apps that display relevant information on the Lock screen, such as email notifications or calendar events.

Hot tip

In the Colors section there is also an option for making the Start Menu, Taskbar and Action Center (Notifications) transparent. This is accessed beneath the color chart for selecting an accent color.

49

● **Themes**. This contains a link to the Control Panel, where color themes can be applied for several elements within the Windows 10 interface.

● **Start**. This contains options for how the Start Menu operates. It can be used to view the Start Menu in full-screen mode and also display recently used items in the Start Menu and on the Taskbar.

...cont'd

Account Settings

The Accounts Settings provide options for adding new online accounts (such as a new email account, or an online storage and sharing service such as Dropbox). They include:

- **Your account**. This displays information about your current account, which will either be the one you signed into using your Microsoft Account details, or a local account, which has no online presence. You can also swap between accounts here.

- **Sign-in options**. This contains security options for signing in to your account. You can create a PIN, Password or Picture password. Whichever method you choose, this will be required to sign in to your account from the Lock screen.

- **Work access**. This can be used to connect to a workplace network, where you can share certain items. To do this you will need to contact the network administrator in order to obtain the correct settings to connect to the network.

- **Family & other users**. This can be used to set up accounts on your computer for other family members, or friends. They will be able to set their own sign-in options and you will be able to switch users by clicking on the Start button and then clicking on the icon of the current user.

The Accounts Settings can be used to switch between a Microsoft Account and a Local account for signing in to your PC.

50

- **Sync your settings**. This can be used to sync the settings you have on your computer with any other Windows 10 devices that you have. For instance, if you have a desktop computer using Windows 10 you will be able to sync settings and apps with another Windows 10 device such as a Surface tablet.

Time & Language Settings

The Time & Language Settings provide options for time zone used by your computer and the format for these items. They include:

- **Date & time**. This can be used to set the date and time, either manually, or automatically, using the **Time zone** dropdown menu. There is also a link to **Related settings** in the Control Panel, where formatting options can be applied.

The date and time can be set within the **Clock, Language, and Region** section of the Control Panel, under the **Date and Time** heading.

- **Region & language**. This can be used to select the language that is used by your computer, e.g. English (United States). You can also add new languages.

- **Speech**. This contains options for how the speech function operates when using Windows 10. This includes the language to use when you are using speech and also the default voice if using apps that speak text from the screen.

...cont'd

Ease of Access Settings

The Ease of Access Settings contain a range of options to help users who have visual or motor issues when using a computer. They include:

- **Narrator.** This can be used to turn on a screen reader so text, buttons and toolbars can be read out loud. You can choose a voice style for the narrator and the speed and pitch of reading.

- **Magnifier.** This can be used to magnify what is being viewed on the screen. The amount of magnification can be increased up to 1600% of the standard view. The color of the screen can also be inverted.

- **High contrast.** This contains options for applying high contrast themes for Windows 10, to make certain elements more pronounced. This can be useful for users with dyslexia.

- **Closed captions.** This can be used by hearing-impaired users to provide text subtitles for items such as movies or multimedia content. The captioning is included in the media and the settings enable you to select color, size and effects for the subtitles.

- **Keyboard.** This can be used to enable the on-screen keyboard and options for keyboard shortcuts and keyboard sounds for when certain keys are pressed, e.g. Caps Lock and Number Lock.

- **Mouse.** This contains options for setting the size of the mouse pointer and also its color.

- **Other options.** This contains options for turning off animations and Windows backgrounds, to make the screen less distracting, and also options for showing notifications.

Privacy Settings

The Privacy Settings can be used to allow, or deny, certain apps access to your location. This can make them operate more efficiently, but you may not want all of your apps to function in this way. They include:

- **General**. This contains options for allowing, or denying, apps access to some of your personal information (such as name, picture and account info), using a SmartScreen Filter to check web pages used by certain apps, send Microsoft information about your typing and allowing websites to provide you with local information based on your default language being used.

- **Location**. This can be used to turn On or Off the location services, to allow, or deny, apps the use of your current location.

The more access you give in terms of your own information and access to apps to share your location, the more unwanted information you may be sent.

- The following options can be used to allow, or deny, apps access to these specific functions: **Camera**, **Microphone**, **Contacts**, **Calendar**, **Messaging**, and **Radios**.

- **Speech, inking & typing**. This can be used to train Windows and the voice search assistant, Cortana, to your writing and speaking styles, so that they can operate more efficiently.

- **Account info.** This can be used to allow apps access to your name, picture and account info.

- **Other devices**. This can be used to view external devices, such as an Xbox, which have access to your apps.

- **Feedback & diagnostics**. This contains options for how feedback is requested by Microsoft. It can be set to automatically, or for a specific time period, such as once a day or once a week.

- **Background apps.** This can be used to specify which apps can receive notifications and updates even when not in use. This includes Mail and the Microsoft Edge browser.

...cont'd

Update & Security

The Update & Security Settings provide options for installing updates to Windows and also backing up and recovering the data on your computer. They include:

● **Windows Update**. This can be used to install system updates, such as those to Windows 10 and also important security updates. They can be set to be checked for and installed automatically (using the **Advanced options** button) or manually using the **Check for updates** button. For some updates, you computer will shut down and restart automatically.

Because of the nature of Windows 10, e.g. it is designed as an online service, there will be regular updates. So check the Windows Update section regularly, even if you have set them to be installed automatically, as you will be able to view the details of installed updates.

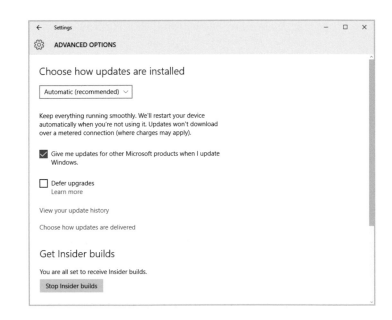

- **Windows Defender**. This contains options for protecting your computer with the Windows Defender app, including real-time protection and also cloud protection for items that are stored online, such as in OneDrive.

- **Backup**. This can be used to back up your important files and documents. It is best if this is done to an external hard drive that is kept separately from your computer. Connect an external hard drive and click on the **Add a back-up location on this PC** button to start the process.

- **Recovery**. This can be used if you encounter problems with the way that Windows 10 is operating. You can select to refresh your computer and keep all of your files intact (although they should always be backed up first); reinstall Windows completely, which will reset it completely and you will lose all of your files and any apps you have downloaded; or return to an earlier version of Windows that was on your computer, without losing any files.

- **Activation.** This can be used to activate your copy of Windows 10, to confirm that it is an authorized version. Activation can be done online.

- **For developers**. This contains options for advanced users involved in programming and app development.

Searching

Searching for items and information on computers and the internet has come a long way since the first search engines on the web. Most computer operating systems have sophisticated search facilities for finding things on your own computer and also searching over the web. They also now have personal digital assistants, which are voice activated search functions, which can be used instead of typing search requests.

Windows 10 has a search box built-in to the Taskbar, which also includes the personal digital assistant, Cortana. This can be used for a wide range of voice activated tasks.

Using the Search box for text searching
To use the Search box for text-only searches, over either your computer or the web:

1 Click in the Search box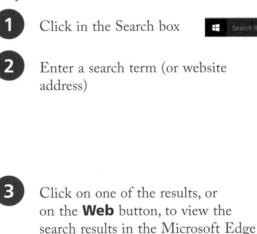

2 Enter a search term (or website address)

Hot tip

The top search result is displayed at the top of the window in Step 2.

3 Click on one of the results, or on the **Web** button, to view the search results in the Microsoft Edge browser

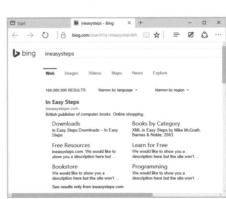

...cont'd

Asking a question

The Search box can also be used to ask specific questions:

1. Enter a question in the Search box

2. Click on the **Search the web** button at the top of the search box to view the results in the Microsoft Edge browser

The magnifying glass icon indicates that a search is going to be undertaken on the web and this will be displayed on a search results page, as in Step 2.

Searching over your computer

As well as searching over the web, the Search box can also be used to find items on your computer:

1. Enter a search query into the search box and click on the **My stuff** button

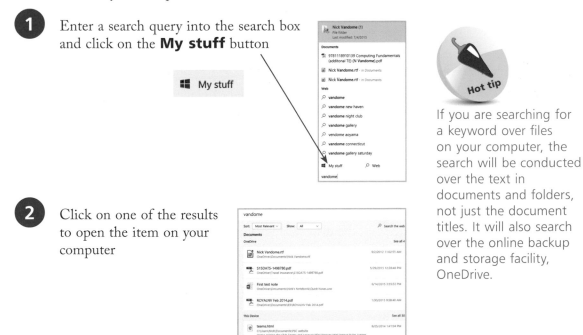

2. Click on one of the results to open the item on your computer

If you are searching for a keyword over files on your computer, the search will be conducted over the text in documents and folders, not just the document titles. It will also search over the online backup and storage facility, OneDrive.

Setting Up Cortana

To ensure that you can use Cortana to perform voice searches and queries, the language settings on your Windows 10 computer have to be set up correctly. To do this:

 Open the **Settings** app and click on the **Time & language** button

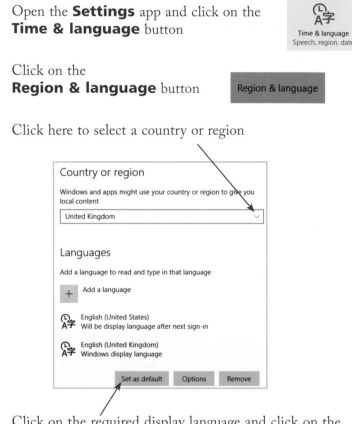

Time & language
Speech, region, date

Click on the **Region & language** button

Region & language

Click here to select a country or region

Country or region

Windows and apps might use your country or region to give you local content

United Kingdom

Languages

Add a language to read and type in that language

+ Add a language

English (United States)
Will be display language after next sign-in

English (United Kingdom)
Windows display language

Set as default   Options   Remove

 Click on the required display language and click on the **Set as default** button

Click on the **Speech** button under **Time & language**

Speech

Select the same **Speech language** as the one used as the display language in Step 4

Speech language

Choose the language you speak to your device

English (United Kingdom) ˅

Don't forget

The county or region, display language and speech language should be the same in order for Cortana to work.

Hot tip

If the Cortana Search box is not displayed once the languages have been set, restart your computer to apply the changes.

Using Cortana

Once the correct languages have been selected for Cortana, you have to ensure that your computer's microphone is working properly since it will be used for voice queries with Cortana.

Setting up the microphone
To set up your computer's microphone:

1 Open the **Settings** app and click on the **Time & language** button

Time & language
Speech, region, date

 (NEW)

2 Click on the **Speech** button

Speech

3 Under the **Microphone** section, click on the **Get started** button

Microphone

Set up your mic for speech recognition

Get started

4 In the microphone wizard, click on the **Next** button

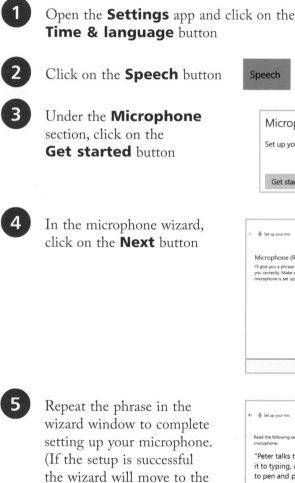

← 🎤 Set up your mic

Microphone (Realtek High Definition Audio)
I'll give you a phrase to repeat so I can make sure I'm hearing you correctly. Make sure you're in a quiet place, and your microphone is set up correctly.

Next   Cancel

Beware

Most modern laptop computers have built in microphones, but an external one may need to be attached to a desktop computer.

5 Repeat the phrase in the wizard window to complete setting up your microphone. (If the setup is successful the wizard will move to the completion page automatically)

← 🎤 Set up your mic

Read the following sentences to complete setting up the microphone:

"Peter talks to his computer. He prefers it to typing, and particularly prefers it to pen and paper."

Next   Cancel

6 Click on the **Finish** button

Finish

...cont'd

Searching with Cortana

As with text searches, Cortana can be used to search over various places and for different items:

1 Click on the microphone button in the Search box to begin a voice search

2 The Cortana symbol is displayed in the Search window with the word **Listening** in the search box. Say what you want to find

It can take Cortana a bit of time to fully recognize your voice and style of speech. Make sure that there is no loud background noise when you are using Cortana.

3 If Cortana cannot understand what you said, you are asked to try again

4 Cortana can be used to open specific apps, e.g. by saying **Open Mail**

5 If the query is general, e.g. **Open Microsoft**, various options will be displayed

6 For a specific request, e.g. **Open Microsoft Edge**, the required app will be opened

Cortana Settings

Settings for Cortana can be accessed from the Search window:

1 Click in the Search box, click on this button (**Notebook**) and click on the **Settings** button

2 Apply the Cortana Settings as required, including an option for Cortana to provide its own suggestions and also setting Cortana to respond to saying **Hey Cortana** from any screen or app

3 Scroll up the Settings window to access more options

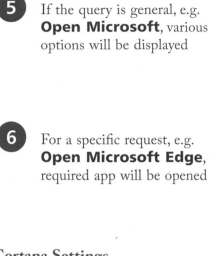

Hot tip

The Notebook within Cortana can also be used to specify settings for a range of cards that are monitored by Cortana. These include items such as Eat & Drink, Events, Finance, News, Sports and Travel. If the options are turned **On** you will automatically receive notifications and recommendations for these subjects.

Setting Reminders

The Cortana Search box can also be used to set reminders, that appear when required. To do this:

 1 Click in the Search box and click on this button in the side toolbar

2 Select on the top toolbar whether the reminder is for a **Time**, **Place**, **Person** or **All** (the default option)

3 Click on this button to add a new reminder

 Hot tip

If the Person or Place option is selected for a reminder, a specific person can be selected from your contacts in the People app, or a geographic location. These can also be used in conjunction with a specific time.

 4 Click in the **Remember to...** text box to add the item for which you want the reminder

 5 Enter the reminder item

 6 Click in the **Time** text box to set a time for the reminder

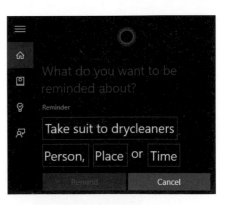

7 Select a time for the reminder by clicking on the required items. Scroll up and down to view more times. Click here to apply the time

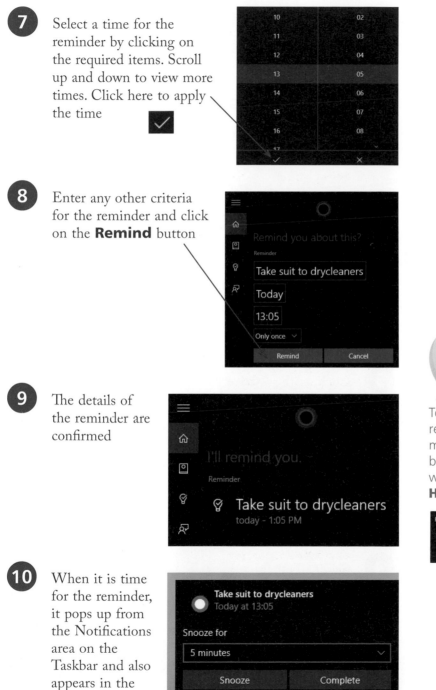

8 Enter any other criteria for the reminder and click on the **Remind** button

9 The details of the reminder are confirmed

Don't forget

To view completed reminders, click on the menu button at the bottom of the reminders window and click on the **History** button.

63

10 When it is time for the reminder, it pops up from the Notifications area on the Taskbar and also appears in the Cortana window

Adding and Switching Users

If more than one person uses the computer, each person can have a user account defined with a username and a password. To create a new user account, as either a Microsoft Account, or as a local account:

1 Access the **Settings** app and select **Accounts**

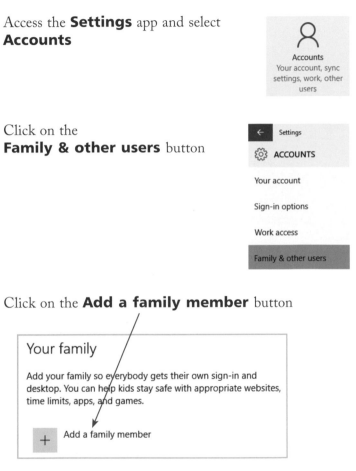

Accounts
Your account, sync settings, work, other users

2 Click on the **Family & other users** button

← Settings

⚙ ACCOUNTS

Your account

Sign-in options

Work access

Family & other users

Beware

The email address is a required field when creating a new user with a Microsoft Account.

3 Click on the **Add a family member** button

Your family

Add your family so everybody gets their own sign-in and desktop. You can help kids stay safe with appropriate websites, time limits, apps, and games.

+ Add a family member

Hot tip

A Guest Account can be enabled within the User Accounts > Manage Accounts section of User Accounts and Family Safety in the Control Panel. Click on the **Guest** button and click on the **Turn on** button to activate it.

4 Select whether the account is for a child or an adult. For a child this provides online security options

Add an adult or a child?

Enter the email address of the person you want to invite. If they use Xbox Live, Outlook.com, Windows, or OneDrive, enter the email address they use to login.

◉ Add a child
Kids are safer online when they have their own account

○ Add an adult

Email address

The person I want to invite doesn't have an email address

5 Enter the name of the new user, an email address and a password to create a Microsoft Account for the user

Let's create an account

Windows, Office, Outlook.com, OneDrive, Skype, Xbox. They're all better and more personal when you sign in with your Microsoft account. Learn more

| Lucy | Vandome |

✓ After you sign up, we'll send you a message with a link to verify this user name.

lucyvandome@gmail.com

Get a new email address

••••••••

United Kingdom

Back   Next

6 Click on the **Next** button to complete the setup wizard

Next

7 The user is added to the Accounts pages

Other users

Allow people who are not part of your family to sign in with their own accounts. This won't add them to your family.

+ Add someone else to this PC

 lucyvandome@gmail.com

Hot tip

Family Safety settings can be applied in the Family Safety section in the Control Panel. It is accessed under the **User Accounts > Manage Accounts** section. Click on a user and then settings can be applied for items such as web filtering, time controls and app restrictions.

65

8 Click on a user to change the type of their account, e.g. from a local account to a Microsoft Account, or to delete their account

lucyvandome@gmail.com

Change account type   Remove

...cont'd

Switching Users

If you have a number of user accounts defined on the computer (several accounts can be active at the same time) you do not need to close your apps and log off to be able to switch to another user. It is easy to switch back and forth.

 Click on the Start Button

 Click on another user's name. They will have to enter their own password in order to access their account, at which point they will be signed in. You can then switch between users without each having to log out each time

As an alternative way to switch users:

 Press **WinKey** + **L** to lock the current user

 Access the login screen for all of the current users and select one as required

Shut Down

When you turn off your computer (see page 33), you will be warned if there are other user accounts still logged on to the computer.

 Click on the **Shut down anyway** button to shut down without other users logging off

Someone else is still using this PC. If you shut down now, they could lose unsaved work.

Shut down anyway

3 Working with Apps

"Apps" is one of the new buzzwords in computing. Put simply it is just another name for computer programs. In Windows 10, some apps are pre-installed, as with previous versions of Windows, while hundreds more can be downloaded from the Windows Store. This chapter shows how to work with and organize apps in Windows 10 and how to find your way around the Windows Store.

68 Starting with Apps

70 Windows 10 Apps

72 Using Windows 10 Apps

74 Classic Apps on the Desktop

75 Closing Apps

76 Viewing All Apps

77 Searching for Apps

78 Pin to Start Menu

79 Pin to Taskbar

80 Using the Windows Store

83 Buying Apps

84 Viewing Your Apps

85 Using Live Tiles

86 Install and Uninstall

88 Task Manager

90 Resource Monitor

Starting with Apps

The word "app" may be seen by some as a new-fangled piece of techno-speak. But, simply, it means a computer program. Originally, apps were items that were downloaded to smartphones and tablet computers. However, the terminology has now been expanded to cover any computer program. So, in Windows 10 most programs are referred to as "apps", although some legacy ones may still be referred to as "programs".

There are three clear types of apps within Windows 10:

- **Windows 10 apps**. These are the built-in apps that can be accessed from the Start Menu. They cover the areas of communication, entertainment and information and several of them are linked together through the online sharing service, OneDrive. In Windows 10 they open in their own window on the Desktop, in the same way as the older-style Windows apps (see below).

- **Windows classic apps**. These are the older-style Windows apps that people may be familiar with from previous versions of Windows. These open in the Desktop environment.

- **Windows Store apps**. These are apps that can be downloaded from the online Windows Store, and cover a wide range of subjects and functionality. Some Windows Store apps are free while others have to be paid for.

Windows 10 apps

Windows 10 apps are accessed from the brightly-colored tiles on the Start Menu (or All apps section). Click on a tile to open the relevant app:

In Windows 10 all apps open directly on the Desktop and their operation is more consistent, regardless of the type of app.

Windows classic apps

The Windows apps are generally the ones that appeared as default with previous versions of Windows and would have been accessed from the Start button. The Windows apps can be accessed from the Start Menu by clicking on the **All apps** button. Windows apps have the traditional Windows look and functionality. Windows apps open on the Desktop.

Windows Store apps

The Windows Store apps are accessed and downloaded from the online Windows Store. Apps can be browsed and searched for in the Store and when they are downloaded they are added to the All apps section of the Start Menu.

The Windows Store is accessed by clicking on the **Store** tile on the Start Menu.

Windows 10 Apps

The Windows 10 apps that are accessed from the All apps option on the Start Menu cover a range of communication, entertainment and information functions. The apps include:

 Alarms & Clock. This provides alarms, clocks for times around the world, a timer and a stopwatch function.

 Calculator. This is a standard calculator that also has an option for using it as a scientific calculator.

 Calendar. This is a calendar which you can use to add appointments and important dates.

 Camera. This can be used to take photos directly onto your computer, but only if it has an built in camera.

 Food & Drink. This contains recipes from top chefs and options for adding shopping lists and meal planning.

 Fresh Paint. An app for creating your own artwork and also viewing photos.

 Groove Music. This can be used to access the online Music Store where music can be downloaded.

 Health & Fitness. This contains options for monitoring your diet and exercise regime.

 Mail. This is the online Mail facility. You can use it to connect to a selection of email accounts.

 Maps. This provides online access to maps from around the world. It also show traffic issues.

 Microsoft Edge. This is the new default browser in Windows 10, replacing Internet Explorer.

 Money. This is one of the information apps that provides real-time financial news. This is based on your location as entered when you installed Windows 10.

 Movies & TV. This can be used to access the online Video Store where videos can be downloaded.

 News. This is one of the information apps that provides real-time news information. This is based on your location as entered at installation.

See Chapter 9 for more information about working with Microsoft Edge.

See Chapter 10 for more information about working with the Calendar, Mail, People and Skype apps and how content can be shared between the different apps.

OneDrive. This is an online facility for storing and sharing content from your computer. This includes photos and documents.

 OneNote. This is the Microsoft note-taking app, part of the Office suite of apps.

 People. This is the address book app for adding contacts. Your contacts from sites such as Facebook and Twitter can also be imported into the People app.

 Photos. This can be used to view and organize your photos. You can also share and print photos directly from the Photos app.

 Reader. This can be used to open and view documents in different file formats, such as PDF and TIFF.

 Reading List. This can be used to save web pages for reading at a later time and even when you are offline.

 Settings. This can be used to access all of the main settings for customizing and managing Windows 10 and your computer. (See pages 44-55 for details).

 Sport. This is one of the information apps that provides real-time sports news. This is based on your location as entered when you installed Windows 10.

 Store. This provides access to the online Windows Store from where a range of other apps can be bought and downloaded to your computer.

 Weather. This provides real-time weather forecasts for locations around the world. By default it will provide the nearest forecast to your location as entered when you installed Windows 10.

 Xbox. This can be used to download and play games and also play online Xbox games.

OneDrive can also be used to share your content, such as photos and documents, with other people. See pages 160-165 for details.

The information for the Money, News, Sports, Travel and Weather apps is provided by Bing.

71

Using Windows 10 Apps

In Windows 8 and 8.1, the newer style Windows apps had a different look and functionality. However, in Windows 10 all of the apps have been created with a more consistent appearance, although there are still some differences.

Windows 10 Apps

Windows 10 apps now open in their own window on the Desktop (in Windows 8 and 8.1 they only opened in full-screen) and they can be moved and resized in the same way as older-style apps:

1 Click and drag on the top bar to move the app's window

In Windows 10 there has been a conscious effort to achieve a greater consistency between the newer style apps and the old, classic style apps.

2 Drag on the bottom or right-hand border to resize the app's window (or the bottom right-hand corner to resize the height and width simultaneously)

Windows 10 Apps Menus

Some Windows 10 apps have their own menus:

1 Click on this button (if available) within the app's window to access its menu

2 Click on the menu button again to minimize the menu to just the icons, without text

3 Click this button to move to previously viewed pages within the app

Managing an app's window

As with older-style apps, the Windows 10 apps also have the same control buttons on the top toolbar:

1 Click on this button to close the app

2 Click on this button to maximize the app's window

3 Click on this button to minimize the app's window (it will be minimized onto the Taskbar)

Classic Apps on the Desktop

The Windows classic apps open on the Desktop, in the same way as with previous versions of Windows, even though they are opened from the Start Menu (or the Taskbar).

Opening a Windows system app

To open a Windows system app:

 Click on the **Start Button** and click on the **All apps** button

 Select the app you want to open

WordPad

The app opens on the Desktop

Hot tip

If apps have been pinned to the Taskbar, as shown on page 79, they can be opened directly from there by clicking on them.

74

 Click on the tabs at the top of the app to access relevant toolbars and menus

Closing Apps

There are several ways to close a Windows app:

1 Click on the red **Close** button in the top right of the window

2 Select **File > Exit** from the File menu (if available)

3 Press **Alt** + **F4**

It is always worth saving a new document as soon as it is created. It should also be saved at regular intervals as you are working on it.

75

4 Right-click on the icon on the Taskbar and select **Close Window**

5 If any changes have been made to the document, you may receive a warning message advising you to save the associated file

WordPad	✕
Do you want to save changes to Document?	
Save Don't Save Cancel	

Viewing All Apps

There is a lot more to Windows 10 than the default Windows 10 apps. Most of the Windows apps that were available with previous versions of Windows are still there, just not initially visible on the Start Menu. However, it only takes two clicks on the Start Menu to view all of the apps on your computer.

1 Click on the **Start** button

2 Click on the **All apps** button

3 All of the apps are displayed. Use the scroll bar to move through all of the apps

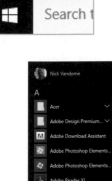

4 Click on a letter heading to view an alphabetic grid for finding apps. Click on a letter to move that section

Hot tip

Click on the clock icon at the beginning of the **All apps** grid in Step 4 to go back to the beginning of the list. Click on the globe icon at the end of the grid to go to the end of the list.

76

Searching for Apps

As you acquire more and more apps, it may become harder to find the ones you want. To help with this you can use the Search box to search over all of the apps on your computer. To do this:

 Click in the Search box on the Taskbar

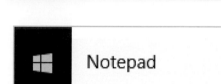

② Enter a word in the Search box

	Notepad

③ As you type, relevant apps are displayed. When the one you are seeking appears, click on it to start the app

Notepad
Windows application

Store

Notepad 8

Notepad Classic

Web

🔎 notepad++

🔎 notepad++ download

🔎 notepad++ free download

🔎 notepad++ download 64 bit

🔎 notepad2

🔎 notepad online

🔎 notepad free

🔎 notepad tricks

⊞ My stuff	🔎 Web

Hot tip

You just have to put in the first couple of letters of an app and Search will automatically suggest results based on this. The more that you type, the more specific the results become. Case does not matter when you are typing a search.

Pin to Start Menu

In most cases you will want to have quick access to a variety of apps on the Start Menu, not just the new Windows 10 apps. It is possible to pin any app to the Start Menu so that it is always readily available. To do this:

 Access **All apps**
(as shown on page 76)

78

Apps can be unpinned from the Start Menu by right-clicking on them and selecting **Unpin from Start** from the menu that appears.

2 Right-click on an app and click on the **Pin to Start** button

3 The app is pinned to the Start Menu. It can now be repositioned, if required, as with any other app (see page 28)

Pin to Taskbar

All Windows 10 apps can be pinned to the Desktop Taskbar (the bar that appears along the bottom of the Desktop) so that they can be accessed quickly. To do this:

1 Access **All apps** (see page 76)

2 Right-click on an app and click on the **Pin to taskbar** button

3 The app is added to the Taskbar

4 Open apps on the Taskbar can also be pinned there by right-clicking on them and selecting **Pin this program to taskbar**

5 Pinned items remain on the Taskbar even once they have been closed

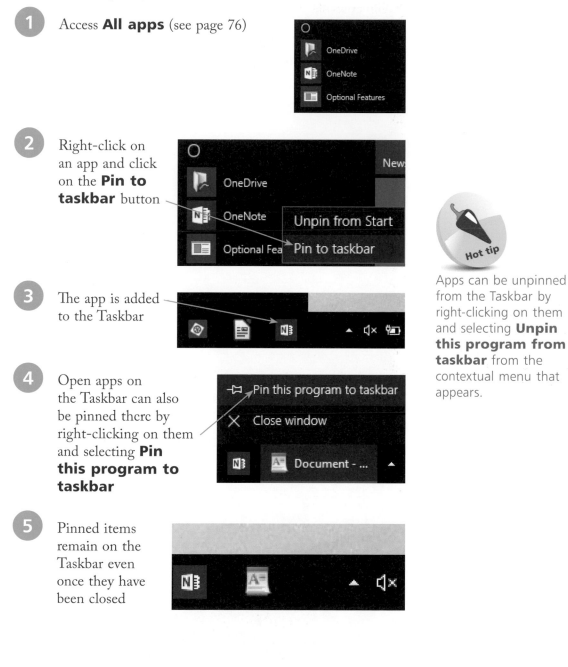

Hot tip

Apps can be unpinned from the Taskbar by right-clicking on them and selecting **Unpin this program from taskbar** from the contextual menu that appears.

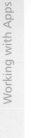

Using the Windows Store

The third category of apps that can be used with Windows 10 are those that are downloaded from the Windows Store. These cover a wide range of topics and it is an excellent way to add functionality to Windows 10. To use the Windows Store:

 Click on the **Store** tile on the Start Menu

 The currently featured apps are displayed on the Home screen

 Scroll up and down to see additional featured apps

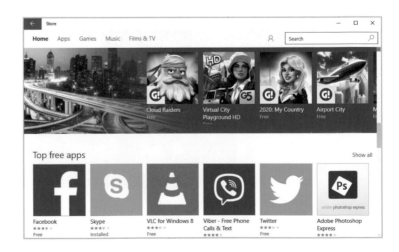

The Windows 10 apps can all be downloaded from the Windows Store.

4 Click on the **App top charts** button on the Homepage and select apps under specific headings, e.g. **Best rated** apps

5 Click on options in the **Refine** section to view apps according to certain criteria, e.g. **Top free**

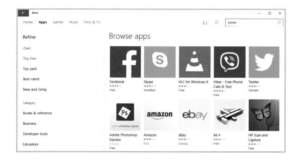

6 Click on an app to preview it

Scroll up and down in Step 6 to view ratings and reviews about the app and also any additional descriptions.

...cont'd

7 Click on the **App categories** button at the top of the Homepage to view the available categories

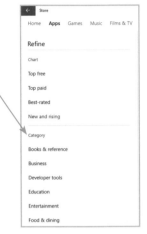

8 Click on a category to access it

9 Click on items in each category to view details about them. Click on the Back arrow to go back up one level each time

Hot tip

To return to the Home screen at any point, right-click anywhere on the Store screen and click on the **Home** button from the top toolbar.

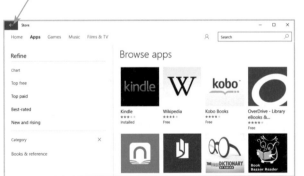

10 Enter a word or phrase into the Search box to see matching apps. Click on a result to view the app

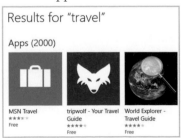

Buying Apps

When you find an app that you want to use you can download it to your computer. To do this:

1 Access the app and click on the **Free (or price)** button

2 The app downloads from the Windows Store. Click on the **Install** button to install the downloaded app

If there is a fee for an app, this will be displayed on, or next to, the **Install** button.

3 The app is added to the All Apps page and has a **New** tag next to it. This disappears once the app has been opened

All apps   New

4 Click on the app to open it and use it (initially it will be available under the **Recently added** section of the Start Menu and also from the **All apps** button)

Once apps have been downloaded they can be reorganized and moved into different groups on the Start Menu, or dragged away from their default group to start a new one.

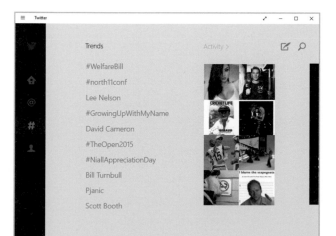

Viewing Your Apps

As you download more and more apps from the Windows Store you may lose track of which ones you have obtained and when. To help with this, you can review all of the apps you have downloaded, from within the Windows Store. To do this:

1 Open the Windows Store and click on this button at the top of the screen

2 Click on the **Purchased** button

> **Nick Vandome**
> nickvandome@gmail.com
>
> _____
>
> Settings
>
> Purchased
>
> My Library
>
> Downloads

3 Your Microsoft Account page opens in the Microsoft Edge browser and displays details of the apps that you have bought and downloaded

| ▮▮ Microsoft | Account | 🔍 🛒 ≡ |

Billing overview

US - Personal account ⌄

Date	Description	Payment Option	Grand Total
7/5/2015	Twitter		£0.00
7/5/2015	Tripwolf - Your Travel Guide		£0.00
6/4/2015	Chef		$0.00
5/12/2015	Picsart - Photo Studio		$0.00

Hot tip

When there are updates for apps that you have downloaded from the Windows Store, this will be indicated in the **Downloads** section, which can be accessed from the menu in Step 2.

Don't forget

You can reinstall apps from the Downloads section, even if you have previously uninstalled them. If there was a fee for an app you will not have to pay again to reinstall it.

Using Live Tiles

Before any of the Windows 10 apps have been used, they are depicted on the Start Menu with tiles of solid color. However, once you open an app it activates the Live Tile feature (if it is supported by that app). This enables the tile to display real-time information from the app, even when it is not the app currently being used. This means that you can view information from your apps, directly from the Start Menu. To use Live Tiles:

1 Right-click on a tile to select it. If it has Live Tile functionality, click on the **Turn live tile on** button to activate this feature

The apps with Live Tile functionality include Mail, People, Calendar, Photos, Groove Music, News, Sport and Money. Some of these, such as Mail, require you to first set up an account before Live Tiles can be fully activated.

2 Live Tiles display real-time text and images from the selected apps. These are updated when there is new information available via the app

3 To turn off a Live Tile, right-click on a tile to select it and click on the **Turn live tile off** button

If you have too many Live Tiles activated at the same time it can become distracting and annoying, with a lot of movement on the Start Menu.

Install and Uninstall

Installing apps from a CD or DVD

If the app you want to install is provided on a CD or DVD, you normally just insert the disc. The installation app starts up automatically and you can follow the instructions to select features and complete the installation.

1 Insert the disc and click on this window

DVD RW Drive (D:) CS5 Design Prem1 ✕
Tap to choose what happens with this disc.

2 Double-click on the **Set-up.exe** file link to run it. Follow the onscreen prompts to install the app

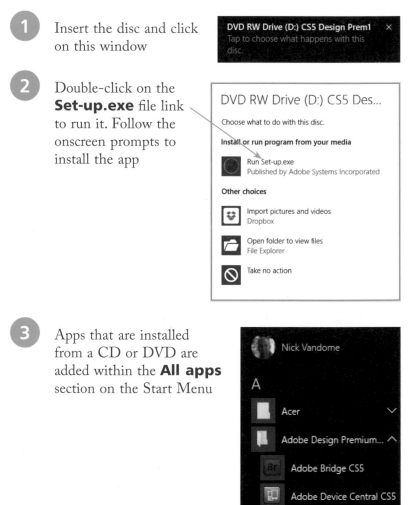

DVD RW Drive (D:) CS5 Des...

Choose what to do with this disc.

Install or run program from your media

Run Set-up.exe
Published by Adobe Systems Incorporated

Other choices

Import pictures and videos
Dropbox

Open folder to view files
File Explorer

Take no action

3 Apps that are installed from a CD or DVD are added within the **All apps** section on the Start Menu

Nick Vandome

A

Acer

Adobe Design Premium... ∧

Adobe Bridge CS5

Adobe Device Central CS5

Adobe Dreamweaver CS5

Adobe ExtendScript Tool...

Adobe Extension Manag...

Adobe InDesign CS5

Uninstalling apps

In some previous versions of Windows, apps were uninstalled through the Control Panel. However, in Windows 10 they can also be uninstalled directly from the Start Menu. To do this:

 1   Right-click on an app to access its menu

2   Click on the **Uninstall** button

3   A window alerts you to the fact that related information will be removed if the app is uninstalled. Click on the **Uninstall** button if you want to continue

Don't forget

4   If the app is a new Windows 10 one, or has been pinned to the Start Menu (or Taskbar), its tile will be removed from the Start Menu. For other apps, they will no longer be available from the All apps option

Some elements of Windows 10, such as the Control Panel, still refer to apps as programs, but they are the same thing.

If apps have been installed from a CD or DVD they can also still be uninstalled from within the Control Panel. To do this, select the Programs options and click on the **Uninstall a Program** link. The installed apps will be displayed. Select one of the apps and click on the **Uninstall/Change** link.

Task Manager

Task Manager lists all the apps and processes running on your computer; you can monitor performance or close an app that is no longer responding.

To open the Task Manager:

Right-click on the Start Button and select **Task Manager**, or press **Ctrl** + **Shift** + **Esc**

Don't forget

As an alternative, press **Ctrl** + **Alt** + **Delete** to display the Windows Security screen, from where you can start Task Manager.

2 When Task Manager opens, details of the currently running apps are displayed

3 If an app is given the status of Not Responding and you cannot wait for Windows to fix things, select the app and click on the **End task** button

Beware

If an app stops responding, Windows 10 will try to find the problem and fix it automatically. Using Task Manager to end the app may be quicker, but any unsaved data will be lost.

4 Click on the **More details** button to view detailed information about the running apps. Select the **Processes** tab to show the system and the current user processes

5 The total CPU usage and the amount being used by each process are shown as (continually varying) percentages

88

6 Select **Performance** to see graphs of resource usage

7 The Performance panel shows graphs of the recent history of CPU and memory usage, along with other details

Alternative View

In addition to the standard view, with menus and tabs, Task Manager also has a CPU graph only view.

1 To switch to the graph only view double-click the graph area on the Performance tab

2 To switch back to the view with menus and tabs, double-click the graph area a second time

3 Select the **Wi-Fi** button in the Performance section to view the activity on your local area network. This tab also offers a graph only view

Hot tip

Resize the window so it does not take up too much space on your screen, and you can see the effects on CPU and memory as you use your system.

Don't forget

If you have a network adapter fitted to your computer, the Task Manager will feature a Networking tab.

Resource Monitor

The Resource Monitor provides an even more detailed view of the activities on your computer, and can be an essential aid in troubleshooting. To start the Resource Monitor:

 From Task Manager, **Performance** tab, select the **Open Resource Monitor** button

Open Resource Monitor

 This displays CPU, Memory, Disk and Network details

 For even more detail, select one of the tabs, e.g. Memory

Hot tip

Right-click any process and choose **Analyze Wait Chain...** to see which tasks are holding up an unresponsive application.

End Process
End Process Tree

Analyze Wait Chain...

Suspend Process
Resume Process

Search Online

4 Basic Controls

Even in Windows 10, much of what you do will be with menus, dialog boxes and windows, as used in numerous versions of the operating system. This chapter shows how to use these elements and how you can control and manage working with folders and files in Windows 10.

92 Menus

93 Dialog Boxes

94 Structure of a Window

95 Moving a Window

96 Restoring a Window

97 Resizing a Window

98 Arranging Windows

100 Snaps

102 Using Multiple Windows

104 Switching Windows

105 Arranging Icons

106 Closing a Window

Menus

Traditionally, windows have a Menu bar near the top, displaying the menu options relevant to that particular window. Some Menu bars consist of drop-down menus and others are in the format of the Scenic Ribbon.

Drop-down menus

For apps such as Notepad and Calculator, the Menu bar consists of drop-down menus:

 Open the app and click, or tap, on one of the Menu bar options to view its details

Scenic Ribbon

For Windows apps, such as WordPad, (and also File Explorer and Office apps) there is a Scenic Ribbon (or just Ribbon) at the top of the window with the Menu bar options:

1 Open the app and select one of the Menu bar options on the Scenic Ribbon to view its details

Some options may have shortcut keys associated with them (e.g. **Alt** + **Up arrow** – Up one level), so you can use these instead of using your mouse. Other examples of shortcut keys are:

Ctrl + **A** – Select All   **Ctrl** + **C** – Copy   **Ctrl** + **V** – Paste
Ctrl + **X** – Cut   **Ctrl** + **Y** – Redo   **Ctrl** + **Z** – Undo

The Menu bar is not always displayed in folder windows. Press the **Alt** key to display it temporarily.

The ellipse (i.e. ...) indicates that if this option is selected, an associated window with further selections will be displayed.

If an option is grayed (dimmed out), it is not available for use at this particular time or is not appropriate.

92

Dialog Boxes

Although simple settings can be made quickly from menu options, other settings are made from windows displayed specifically for this purpose. These are called dialog boxes.

Tabs
Some dialog boxes are divided into two or more tabs (sets of options). Only one tab can be viewed at a time.

Check Boxes
Select as many as required. A tick indicates that the option is active. If you select it again it will be turned off. If an option is grayed, it is unavailable and you cannot select it.

Navigation pane
- [ ] Show all folders
- [x] Automatically expand to current folder
- [ ] Show libraries

Radio Buttons
Only one out of a group of radio buttons can be selected. If you select another radio button, the previously-selected one is automatically turned off.

Click items as follows
- ○ Single-click to open an item (point to select)
  - ○ Underline icon titles consistent with my browser
  - ● Underline icon titles only when I point at them
- ● Double-click to open an item (single-click to select)

Command Buttons
OK will save the settings selected and close the dialog box or window. **Cancel** will close, discarding any amended settings. **Apply** will save the settings selected so far but will not close, enabling you to make further changes.

| OK | Cancel | Apply |

Spin Boxes
Spin boxes let you type or select numbers only. They usually have arrow buttons to allow you to increase or decrease the values.

Number of recent items to display in Jump Lists: 10

Beware

Dialog boxes are usually fixed-size windows and therefore do not have scroll bars, minimize and maximize buttons or resize pointers.

Hot tip

These examples are from the Folder Options dialog box. To access it, select **Options** on the View section of the Scenic Ribbon in File Manager and select **Change folder and search options**.

93

Hot tip

This spin box is from the Taskbar and Properties dialog box.

Structure of a Window

You can have a window containing icons for further selection or a window that displays a screen from an app. All these windows are similar in their structure. This example is for the File Manager.

Forward and Back   Address bar   Search box   Title bar area

Minimize, Maximize/ Restore Close

Command bar

Scroll Up arrow

Navigation pane

Slider

Scroll Down arrow

Scroll bars will only appear when there are items that cannot fit into the current size of the window. Here, only a vertical scroll bar is needed.

If you move the mouse pointer over any edge of a window, the pointer changes shape and becomes a double-headed resize pointer – drag it to change the size of a window (see page 97).

Double-click on an icon to open a window relating to it, in this case a WordPad application window. This window has a Quick access toolbar, Menu bar, Scenic Ribbon, ruler, two scroll bars, and a Control icon at the top left.

Moving a Window

As long as a window is not maximized, i.e. occupying the whole screen, you can move it. This is especially useful if you have several windows open and need to organize your Desktop.

 1 Move the mouse pointer over the Title bar of a window

You will see the whole window move, with the full contents displayed, and transparency still active, while you are dragging the window.

2 Drag the mouse pointer across the Desktop (left-click and hold, or tap and hold as you move)

3 When the window reaches the desired location, release to relocate the window there

If you have two monitors attached to your system, you can extend your Desktop onto the second monitor and drag a window from one monitor onto the other.

Control Menu Move

There is a Move command for the window on the Control menu.

 1 Right-click the Title bar and select **Move,** and the mouse pointer changes to a four-headed arrow

2 Click on the window, holding down the left mouse button and moving the pointer towards the Title bar

3 The mouse pointer changes to an arrow, grabs the window and you can move and drop it as above

If the Title bar has a Control icon, left-click this to show the menu.

	Restore	
	Move	
	Size	
—	Minimise	
▢	Maximise	
x	**Close**	Alt+F4

Restoring a Window

Within the Desktop environment there are a number of actions that can be performed on the windows within it. A window can be maximized to fill the whole screen, minimized to a button on the Taskbar or restored to the original size.

You can also double-click, or tap, the **Title bar** to maximize the window. Repeat the process to restore it to the original.

You can also use Snaps to maximize, move or resize windows (see pages 100-101).

Original size window   Maximize button   Maximized window

You can right-click the Title bar area or left-click the **Control** icon, to display the Control menu (see next page).

Whether a window is maximized or original size, click on the **Minimize** button (left of the top-right three buttons) to reduce the window to its Task button. This will create space on the Desktop for you to work in other windows. When you want to restore the reduced window, simply select its **Task** button.

The middle button is the Maximize button or – if the window is already maximized – the button changes to the Restore button.

Click **Close,** the third button, when you want to close an app or to close a window.

Resizing a Window

If a window is not maximized or minimized, it can be resized.

Drag here to resize horizontally

Drag here to resize diagonally

Drag here to resize vertically

Resize and move all of the windows on your Desktop to organize the layout to the way you prefer to work, or see pages 98-99 for other ways of arranging windows.

1 Place the mouse arrow anywhere on the edge of a window or on any of the corners. The pointer will change to a double-headed resize pointer

2 Click, or tap, and drag the pointer outwards to increase the size of the window, or inwards to reduce the size

Control Menu Size

There is a Size command on the Control menu which makes it easier to grab the edge of the window.

	Restore	
	Move	
	Size	
	Minimize	
□	Maximize	
x	Close	Alt+F4

1 Right-click the Title bar (or left-click the Control icon) and select **Size**

2 The mouse pointer changes to a four headed arrow

3 Click the window, holding down the left mouse button, and move the pointer towards an edge or a corner of the window

4 The mouse pointer changes to a double-headed arrow and grabs the edge or corner, so you can stretch the window to the desired size, then release

Arranging Windows

If you have several windows open on your Desktop and you want to automatically rearrange them neatly, rather than resize and move each one individually, use the Cascade or Tile options.

 1 Right-click a clear area on the Taskbar to display a shortcut menu and select one of the arrangement options

Beware

Only open windows are arranged, not minimized windows. Also, fixed-size windows will get a proportional share of the screen, but they will not be resized.

2 **Cascade windows** overlaps all open windows, revealing the title bar areas and resizing the windows equally

Don't forget

When you right-click the Taskbar, all windows are deselected, so you must click or tap a window to select it and make it currently active.

3 **Show windows stacked** resizes windows equally and displays them across the screen in rows

4 **Show windows side by side** resizes windows equally and displays them across the screen in columns

Hot tip

When you have used a function to arrange windows, a matching Undo function is added to the Taskbar menu.

...cont'd

When you have a number of windows open on the Desktop, you might wish to see what is hidden underneath. For this, Windows 10 offers the Peek function.

1 Move the mouse pointer over the **Show Desktop** area, and open windows are replaced by outlines

This reveals the Desktop icons. To select any of these icons:

2 Select the **Show Desktop** area, and all the open windows are minimized. Repeat to redisplay the open windows

The **Show Desktop** button is on the far right of the Taskbar, next to the notification area.

99

Note that you could instead right-click an empty part of the Taskbar and select the option to **Show the desktop** (which then gets changed to Show open windows).

Snaps

Snaps provide a set of methods for resizing and moving windows around the Desktop.

Maximize Fully

Hot tip

If the window you want to maximize is not the current one, click on it first, before carrying out the Maximize operation.

Click, or tap, and hold the Title bar and drag the window up the screen. As the mouse pointer reaches the top edge of the screen, the window maximizes. The shortcut is **WinKey** + **Up Arrow**.

Maximize Vertically

Don't forget

Alternatively, you can drag the bottom border of the window towards the bottom edge of the screen.

Click, or tap, and hold the top border of the window (until it turns into a double-headed arrow) and drag it towards the top edge of the screen. When the mouse pointer reaches the edge of the screen, the window will maximize in the vertical direction only. The shortcut is **WinKey** + **Shift** + **Up Arrow**.

...cont'd

Snap to the Left

Beware

When you click the Title bar on an app such as WordPad, be sure to avoid the tools on the Quick access toolbar.

To position the window to fill the left-hand side of the screen, click, or tap, the Title bar and drag it to the left. As the mouse pointer reaches the left edge, the window resizes to fill half of the screen. The shortcut is **WinKey** + **Left Arrow**.

Snap to the Right

To position the window to fill the right-hand side of the screen, click, or tap, the Title bar and drag it to the right. As the mouse pointer reaches the right edge, the window resizes to fill half of the screen. The shortcut key is **WinKey** + **Right Arrow**.

Compare Two Windows

Snap one of the windows to the left and the other window to the right.

Restore

Drag the Title bar of a maximized or snapped window, away from the edge of the screen

and the window will return to its previous size (though not the same position). The shortcut is **WinKey** + **Down Arrow**.

Hot tip

Alternatively, to make the two windows the only open (not minimized) windows, right-click the Taskbar, and then choose the option to **Show windows side-by-side**.

Hot tip

Double-clicking or tapping the Title bar will also reverse the maximize or snap. This restores size and position.

Using Multiple Windows

Windows 10 provides even greater flexibility when it comes to working with windows: it is now possible to display up to four windows at a time, rather than just two side-by-side: To do this:

 1 Open an app and drag its window to the left-hand side of the screen, until it snaps left and takes up the left half of the screen

 2 Open a second app and drag its window to the right-hand side of the screen, until it snaps right and takes up the right half of the screen

Don't forget

Apps can arrange in multiple windows in any order, e.g. one can be placed in the right-hand corner and then one on the left-hand side.

3 Open a third app and drag its window into the top left-hand corner of the screen. The left-hand side of the screen will display the two apps

4 Open a fourth app and drag its window into the top right-hand corner of the screen. The right-hand side of the screen will display the two apps

5 If other apps are open when an app is snapped into position, the Task View will display these apps in the space on the Desktop. Click on an app to expand it to fill the available space

Don't forget

Apps can be 'unsnapped' from their positions, by clicking and holding on the top bar and dragging them into a new position.

Switching Windows

If you have several windows open on your Desktop, one will be active. This will be the foremost window and it has its Title bar, Menu bar and outside window frame highlighted. If you have more than one window displayed on the Desktop, select anywhere inside a window that is not active to activate it and switch to it.

Active task button

Active window

Another method of switching windows is to use the Taskbar at the bottom. Every window that is open has a button created automatically on the Taskbar. Therefore, it does not matter if the window you want to switch to is overlaid with others and you cannot see it. Just select the button for it in the Taskbar and the window will be moved to the front and made active.

Move the mouse pointer over a task button, and a Live Preview is displayed (one for each window if there are multiple tasks).

Don't forget

You can click on the preview to select that task and bring its window to the front of the Desktop.

Arranging Icons

You can rearrange the order of the items in your folders or on your Desktop in many different ways.

 Right-click in a clear area (of the Desktop or folder window) to display a shortcut menu

Hot tip

Select the **View** button to cycle through a range of views. Click, or tap, the **down arrow** to see the full set of options.

2 Move the pointer over **Sort by** to reveal the submenu of sorting options and click, or tap, e.g. the **Name** option, to sort all the file icons in ascending name order

3 Select **Name** a second time and the files will be sorted in descending name order

Group By

You can select **Group by** for folder windows (but not for the Desktop). This groups your files and folders alphabetically by name, size, type, etc.

Closing a Window

When you have finished with a window you will need to close it. There are several ways of doing this – use the method that is easiest and the most appropriate at the time.

Don't forget

Save your work before closing any app window in which you have been working. However, Windows will prompt you if you forget.

Open Window
If the top right corner of the window is visible on the Desktop:

 Select the **Close** button on the Title bar

Minimized Window
For a window that is minimized or one that is hidden behind other windows:

 Move the mouse pointer over the associated task button

2 Select the **Close** button on the Live Preview for the task

Control Menu
If only part of the window is visible on the Desktop:

1 Select the **Control** icon (top left corner) or right-click the Title bar

2 Select **Close** on the Control menu

Keyboard
To close any type of window use this key combination:

1 Select the window to make it the current, active window, then press **Alt** + **F4** to close the window

5 Customizing Windows

The Desktop environment is still an important one in Windows 10 and this chapter looks at how to work with it and personalize it to your own requirements and preferences.

108 Using Themes

109 Changing Sound

110 Screen Saver

111 Desktop Icons

112 Screen Resolution

113 Display Settings

114 Ease of Access Center

116 Date and Time Functions

Using Themes

Although more of the personalization options in Windows 10 are now applied through the Settings app, there are still some that can be set within the Control Panel. This includes the overall theme for the appearance of Windows 10.

 Open the Control Panel and click on **Change the theme** link from the **Appearance and Personalization** button

To open the Control Panel, right-click on the Start Button and click on **Control Panel** from the menu.

 Themes apply a co-ordinated color scheme for all elements on your computer

Scroll up in the Themes window to see more options and click on a theme to apply it

 Click on this link on the Themes page to obtain more from the Microsoft website

Get more themes online

Changing Sound

Select **Change sound effects** from **Personalization**,

Personalization
Change the theme | Change sound effects
Change screen saver

to see the name of the sound theme which gets applied to events in Windows

Click the down-arrow on the Sound Scheme drop-down bar to try out a different scheme.

2 Select a Program Event and click the **Test** button to hear the associated sound

If you do not want to have sounds associated with Windows events, select **No Sounds**.

3 Browse to locate a new sound file (file type .wav), then select **Test** to preview the effect

4 Make any other changes, then select **Save As**, and provide a name for your modified sound scheme

Screen Saver

With the screen saver enabled, when your mouse or keyboard has been idle for a specified period of time, Windows 10 will display a moving image or pattern. To specify the image used:

1 From **Personalization**, select the **Change screen saver** button

2 Select the **Screen saver** bar and choose a screen saver, e.g. Bubbles

(None)
(None)
3D Text
Blank
Bubbles
Mystify
Photos
Ribbons

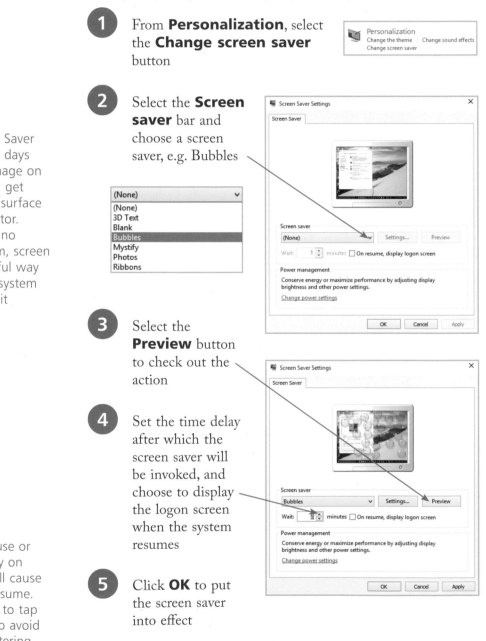

3 Select the **Preview** button to check out the action

4 Set the time delay after which the screen saver will be invoked, and choose to display the logon screen when the system resumes

5 Click **OK** to put the screen saver into effect

Desktop Icons

To control the display of icons on the Desktop:

 Right-click on the Desktop, click **View** and select **Show desktop icons**. A check mark is added

 To resize the icons, display the View menu as above and click **Large icons**, **Medium icons** or **Small icons**

To remove the check mark and hide all the icons, display the View menu and select **Show desktop icons** again

To choose which of the system icons appear, enter **Desktop icons** into the Control Panel search box and click on the **Show or hide common icons on the desktop** link

Select or clear the boxes to show or hide icons as required

You can use the scroll wheel on your mouse to resize desktop icons. On the Desktop, hold down **Ctrl** as you roll the wheel up or down.

Screen Resolution

If you have a high resolution screen, you may find that the text, as well as the icons, are too small. You can increase the effective size by reducing the screen resolution.

Don't forget

If you want to use the Snap function as shown in Chapter 4 you need to have a minimum screen resolution of 1366 x 768.

1 In the Control Panel, select **Appearance and Personalization** and select **Adjust screen resolution** under **Display**

> Display
> Make text and other items larger or smaller
> Adjust screen resolution

2 Click the down arrow next to Resolution and drag the slider, then click **Apply**

Beware

If you have an LCD monitor or a laptop computer, you are recommended to stay with the native resolution, normally the highest.

112

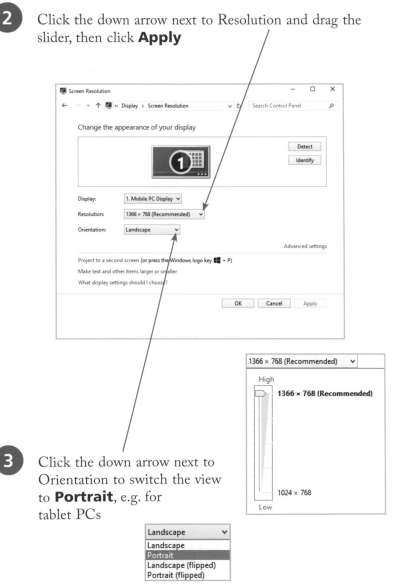

3 Click the down arrow next to Orientation to switch the view to **Portrait**, e.g. for tablet PCs

Display Settings

1   Access the Control Panel and select **Appearance and Personalization** and then select **Display**

Display
Make text and other items larger or smaller
Adjust screen resolution

2   Click on the **use these display settings** link to open the Settings app, where you can alter the size of the text and apps within Windows 10

Display   — □ ✕

← → ∨ ↑ 🖳 « Appearance a... › Display   ∨ ↻   Search Control Panel   🔎

❓

Control Panel Home

Adjust resolution
Adjust brightness
Calibrate color
Change display settings
Project to a second screen
Adjust ClearType text

Change size of items

To change the size of text, apps, and other items, use these display settings. If you want to temporarily enlarge a portion of your screen, use Magnifier. If neither of these makes the changes you want, you can set a custom scaling level (not recommended). Setting custom levels can lead to unexpected behavior on some displays.

Change only the text size

Instead of changing the size of everything on the desktop, change only the text size for a specific item.

Title bars   ∨   9   ∨   ☐ Bold

Apply

See also

Personalization

Devices and Printers

3   Click here to change specific items, such as title bars and menus and click in the size box to select a specific size

Title bars   ∨   9   ∨   ☐ Bold

Title bars
Menus
Message boxes
Palette titles
Icons
Tooltips

4   Click on the **Apply** button to use the selections in Step 3

Apply

Ease of Access Center

Windows will read and scan the list of common tools. Press the **Spacebar** to select the currently-highlighted tool.

The Ease of Access Center allows you to turn on and set up apps and settings that make it easier to see your computer and use your mouse and keyboard.

 1 Open **Appearance and Personalization** and select **Ease of Access > Ease of Access Center**

 2 Click on this bar to get recommendations on the settings that will be most appropriate for you

 3 Otherwise, scroll down to explore all of the settings. Those you select are started automatically each time you log on

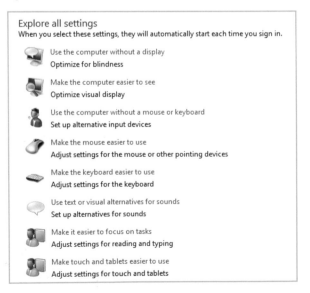

...cont'd

For example, to use the Magnifier:

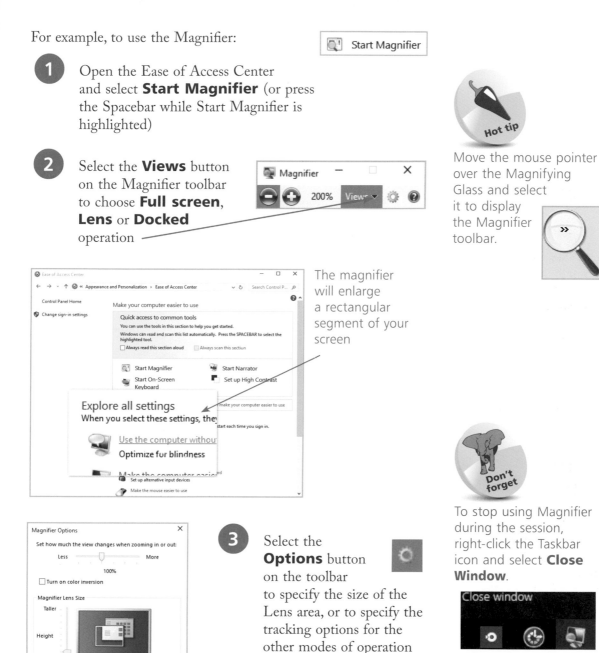

1 Open the Ease of Access Center and select **Start Magnifier** (or press the Spacebar while Start Magnifier is highlighted)

2 Select the **Views** button on the Magnifier toolbar to choose **Full screen**, **Lens** or **Docked** operation

The magnifier will enlarge a rectangular segment of your screen

Hot tip

Move the mouse pointer over the Magnifying Glass and select it to display the Magnifier toolbar.

3 Select the **Options** button on the toolbar to specify the size of the Lens area, or to specify the tracking options for the other modes of operation

4 Select **Control whether Magnifier starts when I sign in**, to turn on Magnifier at start up

Don't forget

To stop using Magnifier during the session, right-click the Taskbar icon and select **Close Window**.

Date and Time Functions

To change the format Windows uses to display dates and times:

1 Access the Control Panel, and select **Clock, Language, and Region**, and then the **Date and Time** option

Clock, Language, and Region
Add a language
Change input methods
Change date, time, or number formats

Date and Time
Set the time and date
Change the time zone
Add clocks for different time zones

2 The current date and time are displayed here

When you select a different locale, the settings appropriate to that country or region will be applied.

3 Click on the **Change date and time** button to set new details

4 Click on the **Change time zone** button to select a new time zone

You can also review and change the way the currency and numbers (including measurements) are displayed.

5 Click on the **Region** option (from the **Clock, Language, and Region** link in Step 1) and click on the **Formats** tab. This can be used to determine the way the time and dates are displayed

6 File Explorer

The File Explorer is at the heart of working with the files on your computer and you can use it to browse all of the information on your computer and on the local network. This chapter shows how you can use the Scenic Ribbon function, modify the views in File Explorer, use the Quick access folder, sort the contents and customize the style and appearance.

118 Opening File Explorer

119 The Taskbar

120 Libraries

121 Scenic Ribbon

123 This PC Folder

124 Quick Access

126 Exploring Drives

128 Address Bar

130 Navigation Panes

132 Changing Views

133 Sorting

134 Filtering

135 Grouping

136 Folder Options

Opening File Explorer

Although File Explorer (formerly called Windows Explorer) is not necessarily one of the first apps that you will use with Windows 10, it still plays an important role in organizing your folders and files. To access File Explorer:

 Click on the **Start** button and click on the **All apps** button. Select the **File Explorer** button, or

 From the Desktop, click on this icon on the Taskbar, or

 Press **WinKey** + **E**, and File Explorer opens with the **Quick access** folder

4 When File Explorer is opened click on the **This PC** link to view the top level items on your computer, including the main folders, your hard drive and any removable devices that are connected

The Taskbar

The Taskbar is permanently visible at the bottom of the screen when working in the Desktop environment. To illustrate the range of functions that it supports:

 Open items are displayed on the Taskbar at the bottom of the window

 Windows of the same type will be grouped next to each other on the Taskbar

 Move the mouse pointer over the File Explorer shortcut to see previews of the folder windows that File Explorer is managing

Move the mouse pointer over the other multiple Task buttons to see the open windows, e.g. for the windows for the Control Panel

119

Hot tip

File Explorer (also known as Explorer) is the program Explorer.exe. It handles the file system and user interfaces, and is sometimes referred to as the Windows Shell.

Hot tip

When you right-click the Desktop, you will find customization functions, Display settings and Personalize on the menu displayed.

Libraries

File Explorer can use the Library for accessing the files and folders on your computer and network. Each Library displays files from several locations. Initially there are five Libraries defined:

- **Camera Roll**, which is the default folder for photos captured on your computer (if it has a camera attached).

- **Documents**, which is the default folder for files such as those created with word processing or presentation apps.

- **Music**, which is the default folder for music bought from the online Windows Store, or added yourself.

- **Pictures**, which is the default folder for your photos.

- **Videos**, which is the default folder for your videos.

Beware

In Windows 10 the Libraries are not visible by default. To show them, click on the **Navigation pane** button and click on the **Show libraries** button so that a tick appears.

120

To view the Pictures Library, for example:

1 Select **Libraries > Pictures** in the Navigation pane

To add another folder to the Pictures Library:

1 Right-click in the Pictures Library window and select **New > Folder**

2 Click on the folder name and overwrite it with a new title

New folder

Portugal

Hot tip

You can also right-click the folder name in the Navigation pane folder list, to display the **New > Folder** menu.

Scenic Ribbon

The navigation and functionality in the Libraries is provided by the Scenic Ribbon at the top of the window. This has options for the Library itself and also the type of content that is being viewed.

1   Click on the tabs at the top of the Library window to view associated tools

Library Tools	Picture Tools

2   Click on the Library Tools tab to view the menus for the whole Library (see below)

3   Click on the content tab (Picture Tools in this example) to view menus for the selected content

Library File Menu

This contains options for opening a new window, closing the current window or moving to a frequently-visited location in the Library.

Library Home Menu

This contains options for copying and pasting, moving, deleting and renaming selected items. You can also create new folders, view folder properties and select all items in a folder.

The **File** button in the Ribbon remains highlighted in blue, regardless of which other menu is accessed.

...cont'd

Library Share Menu

This contains options for sharing selected items, by sending them to the HomeGroup or another user on the computer, burning them to a CD or DVD, creating a compressed Zip file or sending the items to a printer.

Library View Menu

This contains options for how you view the items in the current active folder (see page 132).

Click on the **Options** button on the View Menu to set additional options for the operation of a folder and how items are displayed within it.

Library Manage Menu

This contains options for managing specific libraries. Click on the **Manage library** button to add additional folders to the one currently being viewed.

Library Menu Options

If there is a down-pointing arrow next to an item on a Library menu click on it to see additional options, such as the **Optimize library for** button, which optimizes the folder for specific types of content.

This PC Folder

One of the best ways to look at the contents of your computer involves using the This PC folder. To open this:

 Open File Explorer and select **This PC** in the Navigation pane

Navigation pane   Location   Search box

Hard disk drive

Removable devices such as CD/DVD or USB memory stick

Details pane

The Navigation pane provides the facilities you require to move between folders and drives.

2 Select items and double-click to view their contents

Quick Access

When working with files and folders there will probably be items which you access on a regular basis. The Quick access section of the File Explorer can be used to view the items that you have most recently accessed and also to pin your most frequently used and favorite items. To use the Quick access section:

1 Click on the **Quick access** button in the File Explorer navigation pane so that the right-pointing arrow becomes downwards-pointing

> ⭐ Quick access

✓ ⭐ Quick access

2 In the main window your frequently used folders and most recently used files are displayed

The items displayed under Quick access are not physically located here; the links are just shortcuts to the actual location within your file structure.

[screenshot of File Explorer window showing Quick access view with files including 02_images_win10, 05_images_win10, 09_images_win10, 10_images_win10, clock_new1_win10, clock_new2_win10, Desktop, display_new1_win10, Downloads, Dropbox, ease_access1_win10, quick_access1_win10, Recent folders, skype1_win10, skype1a_win10, skype1b_win10, skype1c_win10, skype2_win10, skype2a_win10, skype3_win10]

To view the actual location of a file, right-click on it within Quick access and click on **Open file location** from the menu.

3 The folders are also listed underneath the **Quick access** button in the Navigation pane

Adding items to Quick access

The folders that you access and use most frequently can be pinned to the Quick access section. This does not physically move them; it just creates a shortcut within Quick access. To do this:

1 Right-click on the folder you want to pin and click on **Pin to Quick access**

Windows 10

> **Open**
> Open in new window
> Pin to Quick access

2 The folder is pinned to the Quick access section, which is denoted by the pin symbol; or

> ★ Quick access
> 🗃 Dropbox 📌
> ⬇ Downloads 📌
> ▭ Desktop 📌
> 🖥 This PC 📌
> 📁 Recent folders 📌
> Windows 10 📌

3 Drag the folder over the Quick access button until the **Pin to Quick access** option appears, and release

Don't forget

To unpin an item from Quick access, right-click on it and click on **Unpin from Quick access**.

Exploring Drives

Explore the contents of any drive from the This PC folder.

 Select one of the drive icons – for example, the **Pen Drive** removable storage device

 Double-click the **Pen Drive** device icon (or select it and press **Enter**) to display the files and folders that it contains

 Double-click a folder entry (e.g. Windows 10) and select one of the files that it contains

Don't forget

Press the **Back arrow** to select the previous library or location, or click the **Down arrow** to select from the list of viewed locations. Click the **Up arrow** to move up one level.

 Double-click the file icon and press **Enter** to open the file using the associated application, e.g. Notepad

...cont'd

You can see all the folder entries in This PC in a structured list.

1 Double-click the **This PC** entry in the Navigation pane

2 The Computer folder is displayed, and the fixed drives plus any removable drives with media inserted are listed

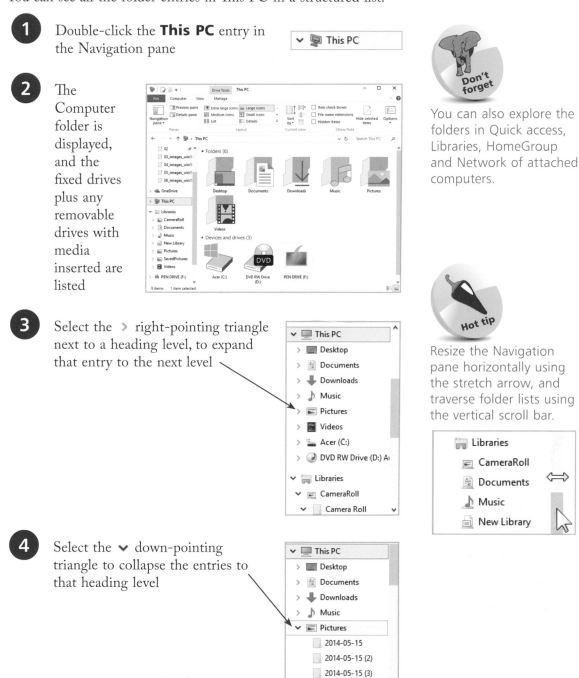

3 Select the > right-pointing triangle next to a heading level, to expand that entry to the next level

4 Select the ⌄ down-pointing triangle to collapse the entries to that heading level

Don't forget

You can also explore the folders in Quick access, Libraries, HomeGroup and Network of attached computers.

Hot tip

Resize the Navigation pane horizontally using the stretch arrow, and traverse folder lists using the vertical scroll bar.

Address Bar

The Address bar at the top of File Explorer displays the current location as a set of names separated by arrows, and offers another way to navigate between libraries and locations.

1 To go to a location that is named in the address, click on that name in the Address bar, e.g. Documents

2 To select a subfolder of a library or location named in the Address bar, click on the arrow to the right

3 Click one of the entries to open it in place of the current location

When you are viewing a drive rather than a library, the Address bar shows the drive and its folders, and allows you to navigate amongst these.

...cont'd

You can specify a new location using the Address bar:

 Click on the Address bar, in the space to the right of the set of names and the full path is displayed

 Type the complete folder path, e.g. C:\Users\Public (or click in the path and amend the values) then press Enter

Hot tip

The path is highlighted, so typing a new path will completely replace the original values.

3 The specified location will be displayed

If you want a common location such as Desktop, just type the name alone and press **Enter**, and the location will be displayed:

Hot tip

You can switch to exploring the internet, by typing a web page address. Windows Edge will be launched in a separate window.

```
←  →  ⌄  ↑  [ ] desktop
                 Desktop
[ ] Music        Search for "desktop"
[ ] Pictures
```

Navigation Panes

The normal view for File Explorer includes the Navigation pane. There is also a Preview pane and a Details pane available.

You can choose different panes to display:

 Open File Explorer and click on the **View** button. This will open the Scenic Ribbon

 The Pane options are located at the left-hand side of the Scenic Ribbon

 Click on the **Navigation pane** button to view this format. This appears down the left-hand side

If you check **Off** the Navigation pane in Step 4, the left-hand panel will not be visible in File Explorer.

 Click on the arrow on the **Navigation pane** button and click here to show or hide the Navigation pane. There are also options here for showing or hiding the Library

5 Click on the **Preview pane** button to view a preview of the folder or file selected in the main window

The Preview pane is particularly useful if you are working in the Pictures library.

6 Click on the **Details pane** button to view additional information about the folder or file selected in the main window

Changing Views

You can change the size and appearance of the file and folder icons in your folders, using the View tab on the Scenic Ribbon.

 1 Open the folder you would like to change and click on the **View** tab on the Scenic Ribbon. Select one of the options for viewing content in the folder

The way items are displayed within folders can also be set within the Folder Options (see page 136).

2 Click on different items to change the appearance of icons

3 Pause at any position, holding the mouse button, to see the effect. Release the mouse button to apply that view

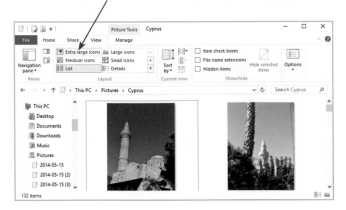

Sorting

Windows 10 allows you to sort your files in the drive or folder by various attributes or descriptors.

 Open the folder, click on **View > Details** and select the attribute header that you want to sort by, e.g. Date

 The entries are sorted into ascending order by the selected attribute. The header is shaded and a sort symbol ▲ added

Select the header again. The order is reversed and the header now shows an inverted sort symbol ▼

 The contents will remain sorted in the selected sequence, even if you switch to a different folder view

Hot tip

Note that any subfolders within your folder will be sorted to the end of the list, when you reverse the sequence. Libraries are an exception, and keep folders at the top (in the appropriate sort order).

Filtering

1 In the Details view (see page 132), select any header and click the **Down arrow**

This shows ranges of values appropriate to the particular attribute and based on the actual contents of the folder. These ranges are used for filtering and for grouping the items in the folder.

2 Select a box next to one or more ranges, and the items displayed are immediately restricted to that selection

3 You can select a second header, Size for example, to apply additional filtering to the items displayed

Filtering can only be applied in the Details folder view.

Size	▼	Tags
3,648 K	☐	Medium (100 KB - 1 MB)
728 K	☐	Large (1 - 16 MB)
6,342 K	☐	Huge (16 - 128 MB)

4 The tick ✓ symbol on headers indicates that filtering is in effect, and the Address bar shows the attributes

> This PC > Pictures > Cyprus > Large (1 - 16 MB) > A – H

Name	⌃	✓ Date	Type

If you navigate away from the folder or close File Explorer, the next time you visit the folder, the filtering will have been removed.

5 Filtering remains in effect even if you change folder views, within the selected folder

134

Grouping

You can group the contents of the folder using the header ranges.
You do not need to select the Details view.

1 Right-click an empty part of the folder area, move over **Group by**, then select an attribute, e.g. **Type**

2 The contents will be grouped, using the ranges for the attribute selected

Any sorting that was already in place will remain in effect. However, you can switch between **Ascending** and **Descending**.

3 Grouping is retained when you switch views (and when you revisit the folder after closing File Explorer)

Select **Group By, (None)** to remove grouping. Select **More...** to add other attributes. The new attributes will also appear in Details view.

4 You can regroup the folder contents by selecting another attribute. This will replace your original choice

Folder Options

You can change the appearance and the behavior of your folders by adjusting the folder settings.

 From the View tab in the Scenic Ribbon, click on the **Options** button and select the **Change folder and search options** link

 Choose **Open each folder in its own window**, to keep multiple folders open at the same time

Folder Options   ×

General | View | Search

Open File Explorer to: Quick access ▾

Browse folders
○ Open each folder in the same window
● Open each folder in its own window

Click items as follows
○ Single-click to open an item (point to select)
    ○ Underline icon titles consistent with my browser
    ● Underline icon titles only when I point at them
● Double-click to open an item (single-click to select)

Navigation pane
☐ Show all folders
☐ Automatically expand to current folder
☑ Show libraries

Privacy
☑ Show recently used files in Quick access
☑ Show frequently used folders in Quick access

Clear File Explorer history   Clear

Restore Defaults

OK | Cancel | Apply

 If you want items to open as they do on a web page, select **Single-click to open an item (point to select)**

4 Select the **View** tab to select options for how items appear in the File Explorer libraries

5 Select **Apply** to try out the selected changes without closing the Folder Options

Apply

6 Select **Restore Defaults** then **Apply**, to reset all options to their default values

Restore Defaults

7 Managing Files and Folders

Folders can contain other folders as well as files, and Windows 10 treats them in very much the same way. Hence, operations such as moving, copying , deleting and searching apply to files and to folders in a similar way. This chapter shows how to perform these tasks and actions while working with folders and files within the File Explorer.

138   Select Files and Folders

140   Copy or Move Files or Folders

144   File Conflicts

145   Open Files

146   Delete Files and Folders

147   The Recycle Bin

150   Create a Folder

151   Rename a File or Folder

152   Backtrack File Operations

153   File Properties

154   Search for Files and Folders

155   Compressed Folders

157   Fonts Folder

158   Character Map

Select Files and Folders

Single File or Folder

 Click the item to highlight it, then move, copy or delete it as required

Sequential Files

 Click to select the first item, press and hold **Shift**, then click the last item, to highlight the range

Adjacent Block

 Drag out a box to cover the files you want selected. All of the files in the rectangular area will be highlighted

Non-adjacent Files

 To select several, non-adjacent files, click one item, press and hold **Ctrl**, then click the subsequent items. As you select files, they are highlighted

Partial Sequence

You can combine these techniques to select part of a range.

 Select a group of sequential files or an adjacent block of files (as described on the previous page)

 Hold down **Ctrl**, and click to deselect any files in the range that you do not want and to select extra ones

All Files and Folders

To select all of the files (and folders) in the current folder, select the **Home** tab in the Scenic Ribbon and click on **Select All** or press **Ctrl** + **A**.

Hot tip

To deselect one file, click it while the **Ctrl** key is being held down. To deselect all of the files, click once anywhere in the folder outside the selection area.

Beware

If you select a folder, you will also be selecting any files and folders that it may contain.

Copy or Move Files or Folders

You may wish to copy or move some files and folders to another folder on the same drive, or to another drive. There are several ways to achieve this.

Drag, Using the Right Mouse Button

 Open File Explorer and the folder with the required files, then locate the destination in the Folders list

 In the folder contents, select the files and folders that you want to copy or move

 Right-click any one of the selection, drag the files onto the destination folder or drive in the Folders list, so it is highlighted and named, then release to display the menu

 Click the **Move here** or **Copy here** option as desired, and the files will be added to the destination folder

Copy here
Move here
Create shortcuts here

Cancel

Drag, Using the Left Mouse Button

In this case default actions are applied, with no intervening menu.

 1 Select the files and folders to be moved or copied

 2 Use the left mouse button to drag the selection to the destination drive or folder in the Folders list – in this example the removable USB storage drive

3 Press **Shift** to Move instead of Copy to another drive. Press **Ctrl** to Copy instead of Move to a folder on the same drive as the source folder

In Summary

Drives	Drag	Drag+Shift	Drag+Ctrl
Same	Move	Move	Copy
Different	Copy	Move	Copy

Open File Explorer and the source folder, then locate the destination in the folder list, ready for moving or copying files and folders.

As you hover over a drive or folder in the Folders list, it expands to reveal the subfolders.

You will see a + symbol if the file is going to be copied, or a ➜ if the file is going to be moved.

141

...cont'd

Using Cut, Copy and Paste

Hot tip

Cut does not remove the selection initially, it just dims it, until you Paste it (see step 5). Press **Esc** if you decide to cancel the move, and the item will remain in place.

 1 Choose the files and folders you want to copy and right-click within the selection

2 From the shortcut menu click **Copy** or **Cut** to move the selection

3 Move to a different folder (or create a new one)

4 Right-click a blank area of the destination folder

5 Select **Paste** from the menu to complete the Copy or move operation

Don't forget

When you Copy, you can **Paste shortcut** (instead of Paste) to insert a link to the original file. However, this is inactive when you Cut files.

Keyboard Shortcuts

Cut, Copy and Paste options are also available as keyboard shortcuts. Select files and folders as above, but use these keys in place of the menu selections for Copy, Cut and Paste. There are also shortcuts to Undo an action or Redo an action.

Press this key	To do this
F1	Display Help
Ctrl+C	Copy the selected item
Ctrl+X	Cut the selected item
Ctrl+V	Paste the selected item
Ctrl+Z	Undo an action
Ctrl+Y	Redo an action

Burn to Disc

If your computer has a CD or DVD recorder, you can copy files to a writable disc. This is usually termed "burning".

1 Insert a writable CD or DVD disc into the recorder drive (DVD/CD RW). Click on this pop-up

> **DVD RW Drive (D:)**
> Tap to choose what happens with removable drives.   ×

2 When the prompt appears, choose the option to **Burn files to disc** using File Explorer

3 Make sure the CD/DVD is selected and copy and paste files into the main window, or drag files there to copy them to the disc, or

4 Select files within another File Explorer window and click on the **Burn to disc** button under the **Share** tab

You can use any of the methods described for copying or moving one, or more, files and folders (see pages 140-142).

File Conflicts

When you copy or move files from one folder to another, conflicts may arise. There may already be a file with the same name in the destination folder. To illustrate what may happen:

 Open the **Documents > Windows 10** folder and the Pen Drive

 Press **Ctrl + A** to select all of the files and drag them onto the Pen Drive, to initiate a copy of them

 Windows observes a conflict – some files already exist, with identical size and date information. Select one of the options

Hot tip

You can, of course, use the Copy and Paste options from the right-click menus, or use the equivalent keyboard shortcuts, and File Explorer will continue to check for possible conflicts.

 If you select the **Let me decide for each file** option, details will be displayed so you can view if one is newer than another. Click on the **Continue** button to confirm the decisions made

Open Files

You can open a file using an associated app without first having to explicitly start that app. There are several ways to do this:

Default Program

1 Double-click the file icon, or

2 Right-click the file and select **Open** from the menu, or

3 Select the file, then click **Open** from the Home section of the Scenic Ribbon. This will open the file in its default app

Alternative Program (App)

You may have several apps that can open a particular file type. To use a different app than the default to open the file:

1 Right-click the file icon and select **Open with**. Pick an app from the list or click **Choose another app** to set a new default app

	Print		
	Move to Dropbox		
Windo 10	Open with	>	Word (desktop)
	Share with	>	Choose another app

2 The same choices are presented when you select the down arrow next to the **Open** button on the Scenic Ribbon in the folder window

Delete Files and Folders

When you want to remove files or folders, you use the same delete procedures – whatever drive or device the items are stored on.

 1 Choose one or more files and folders, selected as described previously (see pages 138-139)

Don't forget

When you delete files and folders from your hard disk drive, they are actually moved to a temporary storage area, the Recycle Bin (see next page).

2 Right-click the selection and click **Delete**

3 Alternatively, click on the **Delete** button on the Scenic Ribbon and click on one of the options

Hot tip

You can press the **Delete** key on your keyboard, after selecting the files and folders, instead of using the menus.

If you choose to delete and then immediately realize that you have made a mistake deleting one or more files, right-click the folder area and select **Undo Delete** or press **Ctrl** + **Z**, to reverse the last operation. For hard disk items, you are also able to retrieve deleted files from the Recycle Bin, and this could be a substantial time later (unless you have emptied the Recycle Bin – see page 148).

Don't forget

You may need to have administrator authority to delete some files or folders from your system.

The Recycle Bin

The Recycle Bin is, in effect, a folder on your hard disk drive that holds deleted files and folders. They are not physically removed from your hard disk (unless you empty the Recycle Bin or delete specific items from within the Recycle Bin itself). They will remain there, until the Recycle Bin fills up, at which time the oldest deleted files may finally be removed.

The Recycle Bin, therefore, provides a safety net for files and folders you may delete by mistake and allows you to easily retrieve them, even at a later date.

Restoring Files

1 Double-click on the **Recycle Bin** icon from the Desktop or in the Navigation pane

2 Select the **Restore all items** button, or select a file and the button changes to **Restore this item**

To see where the Recycle Bin is located, right-click the **Navigation pane** and select **Show all folders**.

A restored folder will include all the files and subfolders that it held when it was originally deleted.

...cont'd

Permanently Erase Files

You may want to explicitly delete particular files, perhaps for reasons of privacy and confidentiality.

 Open the Recycle Bin

 Select the relevant files and folders, then select **Delete** from the one of the menus (or press the **Delete** key)

 Select **Yes**, to confirm that you want to permanently delete these files (completely remove from the hard disk)

Empty the Recycle Bin

If desired, you can remove all of the contents of the Recycle Bin from the hard disk.

 With the Recycle Bin open, select the **Empty Recycle Bin** button

Press **Yes** to confirm the permanent deletion

The Recycle Bin icon changes from full to empty, to illustrate the change.

Bypass the Recycle Bin

If you want to prevent particular deleted files from being stored in the Recycle Bin:

 Select the files and folders, right-click the selection but this time, hold down the **Shift** key as you select **Delete**

| Cut |
| Copy |
| Create shortcut |
| Delete |
| Rename |

2 Confirm that you want to permanently delete the selected item or items. 'Permanent' means that no copy will be kept

Delete File ✕

Are you sure you want to permanently delete this file?

DSC_0051
Item type: JPG File
Date taken: 3/10/2014 5:43 AM
Rating: Unrated
Dimensions: 4608 x 3072
Size: 7.07 MB

Yes   No

Deactivate (or Resize) the Recycle Bin

You can tell Windows to always bypass the Recycle Bin.

1 Right-click the Recycle Bin icon, then select **Properties** from the menu

| Open |
| Pin to Quick access |
| Empty Recycle Bin |
| Pin to Start |
| Create shortcut |
| Rename |
| Properties |

2 Note the space available on Recycle Bin location (free space on hard disk)

 Adjust the maximum size allowed, to resize the Recycle Bin

4 Click the button labeled **Don't move files to the Recycle Bin. Remove files immediately when deleted**, to always bypass the Recycle Bin

Recycle Bin Properties ✕
General

Recycle Bin Location   Space Available
Acer (C:)   678 GB

Settings for selected location
⦿ Custom size:
   Maximum size (MB):   36804
○ Don't move files to the Recycle Bin. Remove files immediately when deleted.
☐ Display delete confirmation dialog

OK   Cancel   Apply

You could also just press the **Delete** key on the keyboard to delete items.

149

Take extra care when selecting files and folders if you are bypassing the Recycle Bin, since you will have no recovery options.

Create a Folder

You can create a new folder in a drive, folder or on the Desktop.

1 Right-click an empty part of the folder window and select **New** and then **Folder**

2 Overtype the default name New Folder, e.g. type *Articles*, and press **Enter**

To create a new file in a standard format for use with one of the apps installed on your computer:

1 Right-click an empty part of the folder, select **New**, and choose the specific file type, e.g. Text Document file

2 Overtype the file name provided and press **Enter**

Rename a File or Folder

You can rename a file or folder at any time, by simply editing the current name.

1 Right-click the file/folder, then click **Rename**, or select the icon and click on the icon name

Hot tip

Use the same method to rename icons on the Desktop. You can even rename the Recycle Bin.

Recycle Bin

2 Either way, the current name will be highlighted. Type a name to delete and replace the current name, or press the arrow keys to position the typing cursor and edit the existing name:

DSC_0870

Paphos1

Don't forget

You must always provide a non-blank file name, and you should avoid special characters such as quote marks, question marks and periods.

3 Press **Enter** or click elsewhere to confirm the name

Preserving File Types

When you have file extensions revealed and you create or rename a file or folder, only the name itself, not the file type, will be highlighted. This avoids accidental changes of type.

Beware

You can change the file type (extension), but you will be warned that this may make the file unusable.

Genealogy Today.txt

Genealogy.txt

Backtrack File Operations

If you accidentally delete, rename, copy or move the wrong file or folder, you can undo (reverse) the last operation and preceding operations, to get back to where you started. For example:

Undo mistakes as soon as possible since you would have to undo subsequent operations first. Also, only a limited amount of undo history is maintained.

 Right-click the folder area and select the **Undo Rename** command that is displayed

The Undo command that is offered changes depending on which operation was being performed at the time.

 Right-click again, and this time there is an **Undo Delete** command for you to select

If you go back too far, right-click the folder and select the available Redo operation, e.g. Redo Rename.

 Now you will have reversed the last two operations, putting the folder and files back as they were before the changes

File Properties

Every file (and every folder) has information that can be displayed in the Properties dialog box. To display this:

1 Right-click the file or folder icon to display the shortcut menu

Hot tip

The purpose of the Properties dialog box is:
• to display details
• to change settings for the selected file or folder.

2 Select the **Properties** option, to display details for the file

3 Right-click a folder icon and select **Properties**, to display the folder information

Don't forget

Click **Security** and other tabs, to display more information about the file or folder, and click the **Advanced** button for additional attributes.

4 Similarly, you can display Properties for any of the Libraries

Hot tip

In View mode on the Scenic Ribbon, select a folder and select the **Options** button. Then select the **Change folder and search options** link to view folder properties.

Search for Files and Folders

If you are not quite sure where exactly you stored a file, or what the full name is, the File Explorer Search box may be the answer.

Hot tip

Open the library or folder that is most likely to hold the file you want. Then click in the Search box to initiate a search, looking at file names and content, limited to that folder and its subfolders.

1 Open a location, e.g. Documents, click in the Search box and start typing a word from the file, e.g. *Nick*

Don't forget

Some files contain the search words in the file names, while others contain the words within the textual content.

2 If that produces too many files, start typing another word that might help limit the number of matches, e.g. *Vandome*

Hot tip

For an attached hard drive, you may be offered the option to **Click to add to index**, and thereby speed up future searches. Indexing is the process of the search facility storing the words that can be searched over.

3 If the location is a drive rather than a library, its contents may not be indexed, so the search may take longer

Compressed Folders

This feature allows you to save disk space by compressing files and folders while allowing them to be treated as normal by Windows 10.

Create a Compressed Folder

 Right-click an empty portion of the folder window and select **New > Compressed (zipped) Folder**

 A compressed folder is created, with default name New Compressed (zipped) Folder.zip

 Rename it (see page 151). You can also open, move, or delete it just like any folder

New Compressed (zipped) Folder

Add Files or Folders to a Compressed Folder

 Drag files or folders onto a compressed folder and they will automatically be compressed and stored there

Windows 10 images

Hot tip

Compressed folders are distinguished from other folders by a zipper on the folder icon. They are compatible with other zip archive apps, such as Winzip.

Don't forget

To create a compressed folder and copy a file into it at the same time: right-click a file, select **Send To > Compressed (zipped) folder**. The new compressed folder has the same file name, but with a file extension of .zip.

...cont'd

Compressed Item Properties

 Double-click the compressed folder and select any file to see the actual size versus the compressed size

Right-click the file and select **Properties** to display this information, if the Details panel has not been enabled (see page 132).

Extract Files and Folders

 Open the compressed folder, drag files and folders onto a normal folder and they will be decompressed. The compressed version still remains in the compressed folder, unless you hold the Shift key as you drag (i.e. Move)

Extract All

 To extract all of the files and folders from a compressed folder, right-click it and then click on **Extract All** or select it from the Extract section on the Ribbon

Extract all

 Accept or edit the target folder and click **Extract**. The files and folders are decompressed and transferred

If the folder specified does not exist, it will be created automatically.

Fonts Folder

Windows includes several hundred different fonts. These offer a wide range of distinctive and artistic effects in windows and documents, and support multiple languages and special symbols.

To view the fonts available on your system:

1 Access the Control Panel and open **Fonts** from **Appearance and Personalization**

2 The Fonts folder is displayed in File Explorer

3 Double-click on a group font such as Arial to see the font styles that it contains

Don't forget

You can also find the Fonts folder within the C:\Windows folder.

157

Hot tip

Double-click on a font to see samples of the characters at various point sizes.

Character Map

As well as letters and numbers, the fonts contain many special characters, not all of which appear on your computer keyboard. You can insert these characters into your documents using the Character Map, or by pressing particular key combinations.

 1 In the Fonts folder select **Find a character** to display the Character Map application

Find a character

Change font size

 Don't forget

Select the **Advanced view** box to display more character set details and to show the Search box, where you locate a character by name.

 2 Select any character to see an enlarged version. The key combination and description is shown on the status bar

 3 Click **Select** to add the character to the copy box, and click **Copy** to transfer it to the clipboard

4 Click the Font box to select a different font from the list, for example Wingdings

8 Digital Lifestyle

Windows 10 makes it easy to work with digital media with the new Photos, Groove Music, Movies & TV and Games apps. This chapter shows how to work with these apps and also the OneDrive function for saving your content online.

160 Using OneDrive

162 Using OneDrive Online

163 OneDrive Settings

164 Adding Files to OneDrive

166 Viewing Photos

170 Editing Photos

174 Groove Music App

175 Playing Music

177 Viewing Movies and TV

178 Playing Games

Using OneDrive

Cloud computing is now a mainstream part of our online experience. This involves saving content to an online server connected to the service that you are using, i.e. through your Microsoft Account. You can then access this content from any computer, using your account login details, and also share it with other people by giving them access to your cloud service. It can also be used to back up your files, in case they get corrupted or damaged on your PC.

The cloud service with Windows 10 is known as OneDrive and you can use it providing that you have a Microsoft Account.

OneDrive was previously known as SkyDrive.

1 Click on the **OneDrive** app on the Start Menu

By default, you get 15GB of free OneDrive storage space with Windows 10 (*correct at the time of printing*). This is an excellent way to backup your important documents since they are stored away from your computer.

2 Click on the **Get started** button

3 Sign in with your Microsoft Account details and click on the **Sign in** button (or the **Sign up now** button to create a Microsoft Account)

160

4 Select the folder that you want to sync with OneDrive and click on the **Next** button (the synced folders will appear in File Explorer and your online OneDrive account)

5 If you want to use OneDrive to access files from other devices (such as a smartphone using Windows 10) check On this checkbox and click on the **Done** button

6 Open File Explorer and click on the **OneDrive** folder. Click on one of the folders to view its contents

Whilst files are being added to the OneDrive folder, this icon is displayed, indicating that they are still being copied:

This icon indicates that all files, or folders, are up-to-date.

Using OneDrive Online

OneDrive is an online service and this enables you to access and manage your files from any web browser with an active internet connection. To do this:

1 Go to the website at **OneDrive. live.com** and sign in with your Microsoft Account details

Click on these buttons at the right-hand side of the OneDrive toolbar to, from left to right: sort the content; display it with its details; as thumbnails; or with the details pane.

2 Your OneDrive content is the same as in your OneDrive folder on your computer. Click on items to open, view and edit them

3 Click on the **Create** button for options for creating new documents or folders. These will also be available from your OneDrive folder on your computer. Click on the **Upload** button to add content from your other locations on your computer

OneDrive Settings

A range of settings can be applied to OneDrive, including adding and syncing folders. To do this:

 Right-click on the OneDrive icon on the Taskbar and click on **Settings**

Click on the **Settings** tab for options for starting OneDrive when you sign in and for unlinking your OneDrive so that it is not linked to the online function

Microsoft OneDrive ✕

Settings | Choose folders | Performance | About

General

☑ Start OneDrive automatically when I sign in to Windows

☑ Let me use OneDrive to fetch any of my files on this PC
   More info

Unlink OneDrive

To sync files with a different Microsoft account, you need to sign out of OneDrive and then set up OneDrive for the other account. After you sign out, your current OneDrive folder will stop syncing with OneDrive.com.

[Unlink OneDrive]

[OK] [Cancel]

Hot tip

If the OneDrive icon is not visible on the Taskbar open the **Settings** app and select **System**. Click on **Notifications & actions** and click on the **Select which icons appear on the taskbar** link. For the **Microsoft OneDrive** option, drag the button to **On**.

163

Click on the **Choose folders** tab and click on the **Choose folders** button to select the folder from your online OneDrive that you want to sync on your computer

Microsoft OneDrive ✕

Settings | Choose folders | Performance | About

Your folders syncing on this PC

If you don't want to keep everything on your OneDrive on this PC, you can choose to sync only some folders by clicking "Choose folders."

[Choose folders]

Don't forget

The option for selecting folders in Step 3 is the same one as in Step 4 on page 161, when OneDrive is initially set up.

Click on the **OK** button to apply any changes to the OneDrive settings

[OK]

Adding Files to OneDrive

OneDrive is built into the file structure of Windows 10 and as well as adding files from OneDrive itself it is also possible to add them to the OneDrive folder from your computer. Once this has been done the files can be accessed from OneDrive from your computer, online or any compatible device, using your Microsoft Account login details.

Adding from File Explorer

To add files from File Explorer:

1 In File Explorer, the OneDrive folder is located underneath Quick access

Hot tip

Your OneDrive folder can be pinned to the Quick access section in File Explorer. To do this, right-click on the OneDrive icon in File Explorer and click on **Pin to Quick access**.

2 Click on the OneDrive folder to view its contents

3 Add files to the OneDrive folder by dragging and dropping them from another folder or by using Copy and Paste

4 The new content is available from the OneDrive app and also online from your OneDrive account

Hot tip

You can share your **Public** folder from your online OneDrive account by opening it and clicking or tapping on the **Sharing** button. You can then email the link to the Public folder to selected recipients.

Saving files to OneDrive

Files can also be saved directly to OneDrive when they are created. To do this:

1 Open a new file in any app and create the required content

2 Select **File > Save** from the menu bar and select a OneDrive folder into which you want to save the file

3 Click on the **Save** button

4 The file is saved into the OneDrive folder and will be available from the OneDrive app and also online from your OneDrive account

Viewing Photos

The Photos app can be used to manage and edit your photos, including those stored in your **Pictures** Library. To do this:

1 Click on the **Photos** app on the **Start Menu**

2 Click here to expand and contract the Photos app's menu

Hot tip

To import photos into the Photos app, click on this button on the top toolbar and select the location from where you want to import the photos. This can be a folder on your own computer; a camera or pen drive attached with a USB cable; or a memory card from a camera inserted into a card reader.

3 Click on the **Collection** button to view all of the photos in the Photos app, arranged by date. Scroll up and down to view the photos

4 Click on the **Albums** button to view photos from specific albums. This includes the Camera roll

Beware

The albums displayed are taken from those stored in the specific folders in File Explorer (by default, the Pictures library). However, the Photos app displays what it thinks are the best photos in the folder, thus creating its own albums.

5 Click on the **Camera roll** button to view photos that have been taken with your computer's camera (or copied into this folder from another location)

Hot tip

To include an existing folder in the Camera roll, right-click on it in File Explorer and click on **Include in library > Camera Roll** from the menu.

...cont'd

6 Within the Albums section, double-click on an album to view its contents. The first photo is also displayed as a banner at the top of the album

Hot tip

The options for where photos are sourced in the Albums section can be specified from the **Settings** button on the Photos left-hand toolbar The default album is **Pictures**, but new ones can be added using the **Add a folder** button. There is also an option for showing photos and videos from your OneDrive folder.

 Settings

7 Double-click on a photo within an album, or collection, to view it at full size. Move the cursor over the photo and click on the left and right arrows (if available) to move through an album or collection

8 Move the cursor over the bottom, right-hand corner and click on the + or - symbols to zoom in or out on a photo

Selecting Photos

Photos within either a collection or an album in the Photos app can be selected and then shared with other people in various ways, or deleted. To do this:

 In Collections, or an open Album, click on this button at the top of the Photos toolbar

 Click here to select a photo or photos

Click on the **Trash** button in Step 3 to delete the selected photo(s).

3 Click on the **Share** button to share the selected photo(s)

4 Click on one of the options for sharing the selected photo(s)

5 Alternatively, click on the **Copy** button in Step 3 so that they can be pasted into another app

Editing Photos

In Windows 10 the Photos app now has a range of editing functions so that you can improve and enhance your photos. To use these:

 Open a photo at full size and click on this button to apply auto-enhance editing effects

 Click on the **Edit** button on the top toolbar to access additional editing options. Click on one of the buttons on the left-hand side to view the options on the right-hand side

3 For the **Basic fixes** option, click on one of the buttons at the right-hand side of the screen to apply that effect to the photo, including Enhance, Rotate, Crop, Straighten, Red eye and Retouch

4 For the **Crop** option in Step 3, drag the resizing handles at the corner of the photo to select the area that you want to keep. The area outside the crop area will be removed

Most photos benefit from some degree of cropping, so that the main subject is given greater prominence by removing unwanted items in the background.

171

...cont'd

5 For the **Filters** option, click on one of the filter effects to apply that to the current photo

Don't forget

It is always worth editing the brightness and contrast of a photo, if only to see if you like the effect. If not, you can undo the action (see Step 11 on next page).

6 For the **Light** option, click on one of the options at the right-hand side to edit the Brightness, Contrast, Highlights and Shadows of the photo

7 For the **Color** option, click on one of the options at the right-hand side to edit the Temperature, Tint, Saturation and Color boost in the photo

8 For the **Effects** option, click on one of the options at the right-hand side to create a Vignette or a Selective focus effect

Vignette

Selective focus

Selective focus enables areas of a photo to be blurred, to create an artistic effect and highlight the main subject. In traditional photography this is known as "depth of field".

9 For the **Vignette** effect, a circular drop-shadow border is created around the photo, to give it an artistic effect

10 For the **Light, Color** and **Effects** options, drag around this circle to apply the effect to a varying degree

11 Click on the **Undo** button to go back one step in the editing process

12 Click on these buttons to, from left to right, save a copy of the edited photo, apply the changes to the original or cancel the editing changes

Groove Music App

The Groove Music app is used to access music that you have added to your computer and also the Music section of the Windows Store, where you can preview, buy and download more music.

 1 Click on the **Groove Music** app on the Start Menu

2 Click on the Menu button to expand the menu so that the titles are visible, not just the icons

3 Click on a category to view those items

Scroll up and down to view the rest of the available content in the Music section of the Windows Store.

4 Click on the **Get music in Store** button to access the Music section of the Windows Store

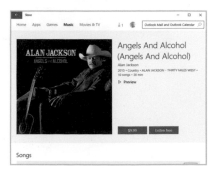

5 Browse through the store with the categories in the main window. Click on an item to preview it

Music that has been bought in the Music section of the Windows Store is then available to be played within the Groove Music app.

6 Once you have selected an item, you can preview individual tracks, view information about the artist and buy albums or specific tracks

Playing Music

Playing your own music

Music that has been added to your computer can be played through the Groove Music app, and you can automatically specify new music to be included when it is added. To do this:

1 Open the Groove Music app and click on either the **Albums**, **Artists**, or **Songs** buttons

- ◎ Albums
- ☐ Artists
- ♫ Songs

2 Click on the **Change where we look** link to specify where the Groove Music app looks for music on your computer

All done! We've added the music from this PC.
Change where we look

3 Click on this button to add a new location from where music can be added to the Groove Music app

Build your collection from your local music files
Right now, we're watching these folders:

| Music C:\Users\Nick\OneDrive\Music | × |

| Music C:\Users\Public\Music | × | Music C:\Users\Nick\Music | × |

Done

4 Click on the **Done** button

5 Items from the locations selected in Step 3 are displayed under the categories buttons. For albums, click on an item to view all of its tracks

175

Hot tip

You can also add music to the Groove Music app or the Library that you have stored in your OneDrive folder.

Hot tip

When a folder is added to the Music library, any music that is copied here will be displayed by the Groove Music app.

...cont'd

6 Double-click on an individual track to play it or click on the **Play** button to play a whole album

Beware

Do not copy music and use it for commercial purposes as this will infringe the copyright of the artist.

7 This button is displayed next to the currently playing track and its details are displayed at the bottom of the Groove Music app's window

8 Drag this button to move through the current track

9 Use these buttons to, from left to right: go to the start of a track; pause/play a track; go to the end of a track; change, or mute, the volume; shuffle the available tracks; or repeat a track

Viewing Movies and TV

For movie and TV lovers, the Movies & TV app performs a similar function to the Groove Music app. It connects to the Windows Store from where you can preview and buy your favorite movies and TV shows.

1 Click on the **Movies & TV** app on the Start Menu

2 Click on the Menu button to view the titles for each menu button (in the same way as for the Groove Music app)

3 Click on the **Shop for more** button to access the **Movies & TV** section of the Windows Store

4 Click on an item to see more information, view a preview clip, buy, or rent, and download the movie

Beware

By default, DVDs cannot be played on Windows 10 computers. To do this you have to download and buy an enhanced version of the Windows Media Player from the Microsoft website.

Don't forget

You can add your own video clips to the Movies & TV app, from the Videos library in File Explorer, in the same way as adding your own music to the Groove Music app.

Playing Games

The Xbox app can be used with the Xbox 360 games console. It can be used to play games, join friends for multi-player games, watch TV shows and movies and listen to music. It links to a number of services so that you can access content from websites such as YouTube and Netflix. To use the Xbox app:

 Click on the **Xbox** app on the Start Menu

 You have to log in with your Microsoft Account details in order to play Xbox games and interact with other users. Click on the **Click here to sign in** link

3 Enter your Microsoft Account details and click on the **Sign in** button

You can also log in to the Xbox site at **www.xbox.com** to download games and find other people with whom to play games.

4 Click on games to play them and click on these buttons to view your scores and interact with other players

9 Microsoft Edge Browser

Microsoft Edge is the first new web browser that Microsoft has produced in a generation. It is fast and responsive and has a range of innovative features. This chapter looks at how to use the Edge browser to open web pages, use tabs and bookmarks and add notes and graphics to pages.

180 Internet Connection

182 Introducing the Edge Browser

183 Smart Address Bar

184 Setting a Homepage

185 Using Tabs

186 Bookmarking Web Pages

187 Adding Notes to Web Pages

189 Sharing Notes and Clippings

190 Organizing with the Hub

192 Reading List

193 Reading View

194 Menu Options

Internet Connection

Before you can use the internet and browse the web, your computer needs to be set up for connection to the internet. To do this you will require:

- An Internet Service Provider (ISP), to provide an account that gives you access to the internet.

- A transmission network – cable, telephone or wireless.

- Some hardware to link into that transmission network.

- For a broadband connection, such as Digital Subscriber Line (DSL) or cable, you need a DSL or Cable modem or router, usually provided by the ISP.

- For dial-up connection, you need a dial-up modem, which is usually pre-installed on your computer.

Your ISP may provide software to help you set up your hardware, configure your system and register your ISP account details. However, if you are required to install the connection or, if you are configuring a second connection as a backup, you can use the Set Up a Connection or Network wizard.

1 Access the **Control Panel** and open the **Network and Internet** section and select the **View network status and tasks** link, under the **Network and Sharing Center** heading

Network and Sharing Center
View network status and tasks | Connect to a network
View network computers and devices

2 Click on the **Set up a new connection or network** link to display the connection options supported

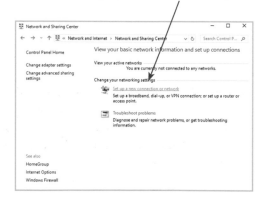

3 Select **Connect to the Internet** and click **Next**

Set Up a Connection or Network

Choose a connection option

Connect to the Internet
Set up a broadband or dial-up connection to the Internet.

Set up a new network
Set up a new router or access point.

Connect to a workplace
Set up a dial-up or VPN connection to your workplace.

Next   Cancel

4 The **Connect to the Internet** wizard launches. Select the appropriate connection method from those offered

Connect to the Internet

How do you want to connect?

Broadband (PPPoE)
Connect using DSL or cable that requires a user name and password.

☐ Show connection options that this computer is not set up to use

Cancel

Windows identifies all of the possible connection methods based on the hardware configuration of your computer. If you have a wireless router or network, you may have an option for wireless connection. If there is no dial-up modem installed, then the Dial-up connection method will not be offered.

Beware

If Windows has already recognized your connection, it detects this. You can select **Browse the Internet now** or **Set up a second connection** (e.g. as a backup).

You are already connected to the Internet

→ Browse the Internet now

Don't forget

Continue through the wizard to complete the set-up of your Internet connection, ready to start browsing the Internet.

Internet Explorer can still be used with Windows 10 and it will probably continue to be supported for a considerable period of time.

The Start page also displays news information.

The Start page can be replaced by your own specific Homepage, see page 184 for details.

Introducing the Edge Browser

The web browser Internet Explorer (IE) has been synonymous with Microsoft for almost as long as the Windows operating system. Introduced in 1995, shortly after Windows 95, it has been the default browser for a generation of web users. However, as with most technologies, the relentless march of time has caught up with IE and, although it is still included with Windows 10, the preferred browser is a new one, designed specifically for the digital mobile age. It is called Microsoft Edge and adapts easily to whichever environment it is operating in: desktop, tablet or phone.

The Microsoft Edge browser has a number of performance and speed enhancements from IE and it also recognizes that modern web users want a lot more from their browser than simply being able to look at web pages. It includes a function for drawing on and annotating web pages, which can then be sent to other people as screenshots.

There is also a Hub where you can store all of your favorites, downloads and pages that you have selected to read at a later date (which can be when you are offline if required).

Click on this icon from the **Taskbar** or the **All apps** menu to open the Microsoft Edge browser at the default Start page.

Back/forward buttons   Refresh   Toolbar buttons

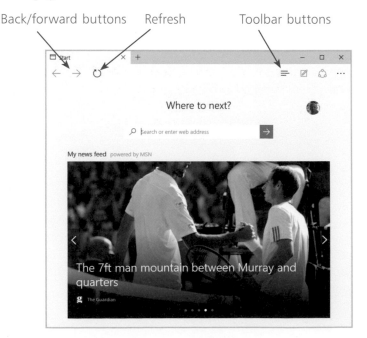

Smart Address Bar

Smart address bars are now a familiar feature in a lot of modern browsers and Microsoft Edge is no different. This can be used to enter a specific web address, to open that page, or use it to search for a word or phrase. To use the smart address bar:

1 Click anywhere in the Start page address box or in the address box at the top of a web page

2 Start typing a word or website address. As you type, options appear below the address bar. Click on one of the options under **Sites** to go to a specific web page

The digital assistant, Cortana, can also be used to open web pages, by asking it to open a specific page. The page will be opened in Microsoft Edge.

183

3 Click on one of the options under **Search suggestions** to go to a page with those search results

Setting a Homepage

By default, Microsoft Edge opens at its own Start page. This may not be ideal for most users, who will want to set their own Homepage that appears when Microsoft Edge is launched.

1 Click on this button on the top toolbar to access the menu options

2 Click on the **Settings** button

3 By default, the Start page is selected as the opening page

Hot tip

Within the settings for Microsoft Edge there is an option for importing favorites from another web browser. To do this, click on the **Import favorites from another browser** button, select the required browser and click on the **Import** button.

SETTINGS

Choose a theme

Light	∨

Show the favorites bar

⬤ Off

Import favorites from another browser

Open with

⦿ Start page

◯ New tab page

◯ Previous pages

◯ A specific page or pages

4 Click on the **A specific page or pages** radio button

5 Click on the **Custom** button

Don't forget

If a specific Homepage is assigned, the Start page as shown on page 182 will not be displayed.

⦿ A specific page or pages

MSN

Bing

Custom

6 Enter the website address you want to use as your Homepage and click on the **+** button

ineasysteps.com	×

+

Using Tabs

Being able to open several web pages at the same time in different tabs is now a common feature of web browsers. To do this with Microsoft Edge:

 1 Click on this button at the top of Microsoft Edge window

2 Pages can be opened in new tabs using the smart address bar or the list of **Top sites** that appears below it

Hot tip

The Start page for new tabs, as displayed in Step 2, can be changed, if required. To do this, open the Microsoft Edge Settings as shown on the previous page and change the selection under the **Open new tabs with** heading.

3 All open tabs are displayed at the top of the window. Click and hold on a tab to drag it into a new position

Bookmarking Web Pages

Your favorite web pages can be bookmarked so that you can access them with one click from the Hub area, rather than having to enter the web address each time. To do this:

 Open the web page that you want to bookmark

 Click on this button on the toolbar

 Click on the **Favorites** button

 Enter a name for the favorite and where you want it to be saved to (click on the **Create new folder** link if you want to save it to a new location)

The Favorites bar can be displayed underneath the Address bar by opening the Microsoft Edge Settings and dragging the **Show the favorites bar** button to **On**.

 Click on the **Add** button

 The star button turns yellow, indicating that the web page has been added as a favorite

7 Click on this button to access your favorites (see page 190)

Adding Notes to Web Pages

One of the innovations in the Microsoft Edge browser is the ability to draw on and annotate web pages. This can be useful to highlight parts of a web page or add your own comments and views, which can then be sent to other people. To add notes:

1 Open a web page to which you want to add a note, or draw on and click on this button on the toolbar of the Microsoft Edge browser

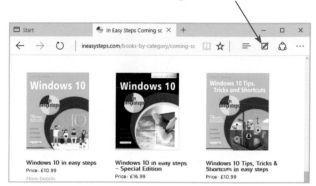

2 Click on one of the pen options

3 Click on the small triangle in the bottom right-hand corner to select formatting and shape options for the pen

Click on this button on the Notes toolbar to create a web clipping. This an area of a web page that is selected by dragging over it to make the selection. Web clippings can be shared in the same way as notes.

Click on this button on the Notes toolbar to Save a web note or a clipping. These can then be accessed from the Favorites section of Microsoft Edge (.see page 190).

...cont'd

 Click and drag on the web page to draw over it

188

 Click on the eraser icon and drag over any items that you have drawn to remove them, or part of them

 Click on the text icon to add your own text

 Drag over the web page to create a text box

 Type the text that you want displayed on the web page

This is the one I mentioned.

Click and drag here on a text box to move its position

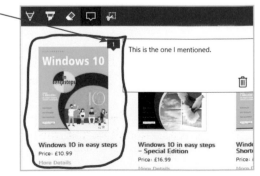

Sharing Notes and Clippings

Once you have created a web note, this can be saved or shared with other people. There is also an option for selecting part of a web page and sharing this too.

Sharing a web note
To share a web note with other people:

1 Once the web note is finished, click on this button on the toolbar to share the web note

2 Select an app with which you want to share the web note

The process for sharing a web clipping is the same as for a web note.

3 The web note is displayed in the selected app

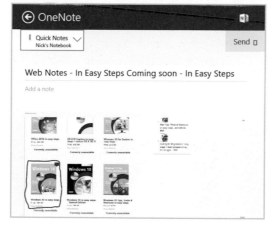

4 Click on the **Send** button to send the web note to the app

Organizing with the Hub

The Hub is the area where you can store a variety of items for the Microsoft Edge browser; from your favorite web pages to pages that you want to read offline at a later date. To use the Hub:

1 Click on this button to open the Hub

2 Click on this button to view your favorites. Click on one to go to that page

The Favorites window also has an option for importing favorites from other web browsers. Click on the **Import favorites** link, select the required browser and click on the **Import** button.

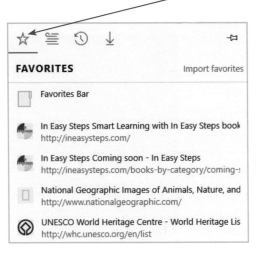

3 Click on this button to view your Reading List of pages that you have saved to read offline, or at a later date

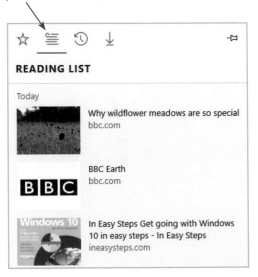

4 Click on this button to view your web browsing history

Browsing data can also be cleared from within Microsoft Edge settings. Under **Clear browsing data**, click on the **Choose what to clear** button, check **On** all of the items you want to clear and click on the **Clear** button.

5 Click on **Clear all history** to remove the items in the history

Clear all history

6 Click on this button to view items that you have downloaded from the web, such as PDF documents or apps (although not those from the Windows Store)

DOWNLOADS   Open folder

Past Downloads	Clear all
Product-Backlog.xlsx ineasysteps.com	×
Communication-Plan.docx ineasysteps.com	×
Building-Android-Apps-codes.zip ineasysteps.com	×

Reading List

With some web pages you may want to save the content so that you can read it at a later date. If you make the page a favorite, the content could change the next time you look at it. Instead, you can add the page to your Reading List to ensure that you can read the same content. Also, this has the advantage that you can access the items in your Reading List when you are offline and not connected to the internet. To do this:

 Open the web page that you want to add to the Reading List

 Click on this button on the Microsoft Edge toolbar

 Click on the **Reading list** button

Hot tip

The Reading List is an excellent option if you are traveling and do not have internet access. You can save numerous articles in the Reading List and access them even when you are offline.

192

 Enter a name for the item and click on the **Add** button

 Click on this button within the Hub to access and view your Reading List items

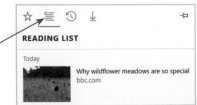

Reading View

Modern web pages contain a lot more items than just text and pictures: video clips, pop-up ads, banners and more contribute to the multimedia effect on many web pages. At times this additional content can enhance the page, but a lot of the time it is a distraction. If you want to just concentrate on the main item on a web page you can do this with the Reading View function:

 Open the web page that you want to view in Reading View

 Click on this button on the Microsoft Edge toolbar

3 The text and pictures are presented on a new page, with any additional content removed

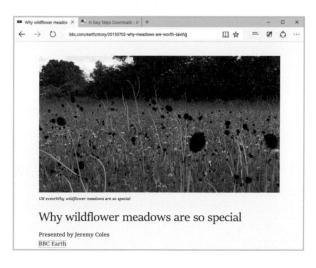

Not all web pages support the Reading View functionality. If it is not supported, the button in Step 2 will be grayed-out.

4 Click on this button to return to the standard page view

Menu Options

There is no traditional menu bar in Microsoft Edge, but menu options can be accessed from the right-hand toolbar:

 Click on this button to access the menu items

 Click here to open a new browsing window, or a **New InPrivate window** which does not record any of your browsing history

New window	
New InPrivate window	
Zoom	— 100% +
Find on page	
Print	
Pin to Start	
F12 Developer Tools	
Open with Internet Explorer	
Send feedback	
Settings	

 Click on the **Zoom** button to increase or decrease the magnification of the page being viewed

The full range of Microsoft Edge **Settings** can be accessed from the menu button.

194

Click on the **Find on page** button to search for a specific word or phrase on the web page

Click on the **Print** button to print the current web page

Click on the **Open with Internet Explorer** button to open the current web page in Microsoft Edge's predecessor

10 Keeping in Touch

This chapter looks at communicating via the Mail, People, Skype and Calendar apps.

196 Setting Up Mail

198 Working with Mail

200 Finding People

204 Chatting with Skype

206 Using the Calendar

Setting Up Mail

Email has become an essential part of everyday life, both socially and in the business world. Windows 10 accommodates this with the Mail app. This can be used to link to online services such as Gmail and Outlook (the renamed version of Hotmail) and also other email accounts. To set up an email account with Mail:

 Click on the **Mail** app on the Start Menu

2 Click on the **Get started** button

3 Click on the **Add account** button

The **Other account** option in Step 4 can be used to add a non-webmail account. This is usually a POP3 account and you will need your email address, username, password, and usually the incoming and outgoing email servers. If you do not know these they should be supplied by your email provider. They should also be available in the Accounts settings of the email app you want to add to the Mail app.

4 Select the type of account to which you want to link via the Mail app. This can be an online email account that you have already set up

5 Enter your current login details for the selected email account and click on the **Sign-in** button

iCloud

Email address

nickvandome@mac.com

Password

••••••••

We'll save this information, so you don't have to sign in every time.

Cancel   Sign-in   ...

You can add more than one account to the Mail app. If you do this you will be able to select the different accounts to view within Mail.

6 Once it has been connected, the details of the account are shown under the Mail heading, including the mailboxes within the account. Click on the **Inbox** to view the emails within it

7 The list of emails appear in the left-hand pane. Double-click on an email to view it at full size

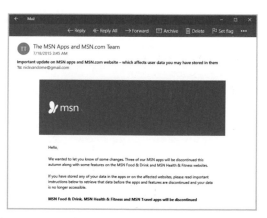

By default, the main window displays the item that was most recently selected in your Inbox.

197

Working with Mail

Once you have set up an account in the Mail app you can then start creating and managing your emails with it.

1 On the Inbox page, open an email and click on the **Reply**, **Reply All** or **Forward** buttons to respond

← Reply   ≪ Reply All   → Forward

2 Open an email and click on the **Delete** button to remove it

🗑 Delete

Composing email

To compose and send an email message:

1 Click on this button to create a new message

+ New mail

2 Click in the **To** field and enter an email address

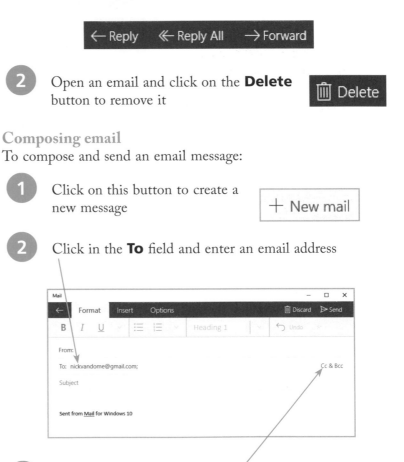

3 Click on the **Cc & Bcc** link to access options for blind copying

4 The email address can either be in the format of myname@gmail.com or enter the name of one of your contacts in the People app and the email address will be entered automatically

Don't forget

Contacts that are added automatically as email recipients are taken from the People app, providing there is an email address connected to their entry.

198

5 Enter a subject heading and body text to the email

Nice sunset!

Hi, here's one that I took earlier!

Sent from Mail for Windows 10

6 Click on the **Insert** button on the top toolbar in the new email window and select one of the options, such as **Pictures**

Mail

← Format Insert Options

Attach Table Pictures Link

7 Click on a folder from which you want to attach the file and click on the **Insert** button

Insert

Open

← → ∨ ↑ > Libraries > Pictures > Malta

Organize ▾ New folder

Downloads
Music
Pictures
Videos
Acer (C:)

DSC_0134 DSC_0135

8 The file is shown in the body of the email

Nice sunset!

Hi, here's one that I took earlier!

Sent from Mail for Windows 10

9 Select an item of text and select the text formatting options from the top toolbar

B *I* U ∨ ≡¶ Heading 1 ∨ ↶ Undo

10 Click on this button to send the email

▷ Send

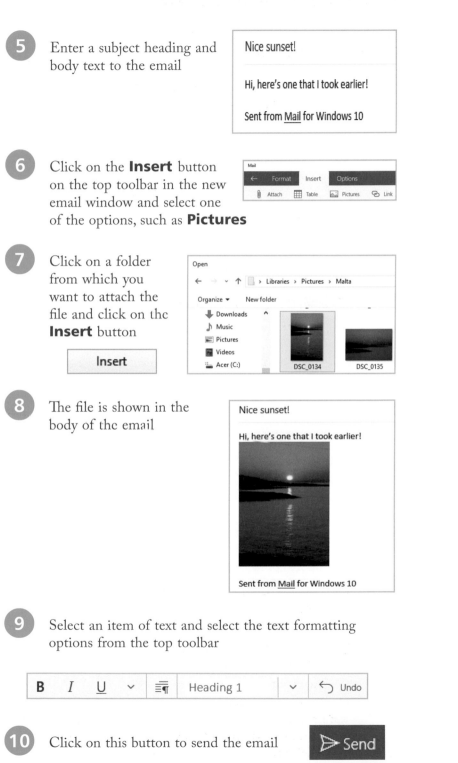

Finding People

An electronic address book is always a good feature to have on a computer and with Windows 10 this function is provided by the People app. This not only allows you to add your own contacts manually, you can also link to any of your online accounts, such as Facebook, Twitter and LinkedIn, and import the contacts that you have there. To do this:

1 Click on the **People** app on the Start Menu

2 The current contacts are displayed. (By default, these will be linked to your Microsoft Account, if you have created one)

Hot tip

You can also select accounts to add to the People app from the Homepage when you first open it.

3 Click on this button and click on the **Settings** button to add new accounts from which you want to import contacts

Don't forget

Click on the **Get social apps** button in Step 4 to download apps such as Twitter and Facebook, which can then be used to link to your contacts in these apps.

4 Click on the **Add an account** button

...cont'd

5 Select the account or service from which you would like to import your contacts

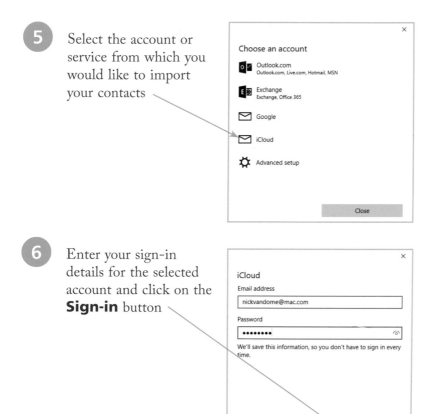

6 Enter your sign-in details for the selected account and click on the **Sign-in** button

7 A confirmation window informs you that the account has been set up and linked to the People app. Click on the **Done** button

All done!

Your account was set up successfully.

✉ nickvandome@mac.com

Done

8 The contacts from the linked account are imported and added under the **Contacts** heading

9 Click on a contact to view its details

Don't forget

See page 203 for details about editing an entry.

201

...cont'd

Adding contacts manually

As well as importing contacts, it is also possible to enter them manually into the People app:

1 Click on this button at the top of the **People** app

2 Enter details for the new contact, including name, email address and phone number

Hot tip

To delete a contact, right-click on their name in the Contacts list and click on the **Delete** button to remove it.

3 Click on the arrow next to a field to access additional options for that item

4 Click on the **Save** button at the top of the window to create the new contact

...cont'd

5 Click on a contact in the Contacts window to view their details

6 To edit a contact's details, click on the **Edit** button. This brings up the same window as in Step 2, on the previous page, where the details can be edited

The photo for your own details within the People app is taken from your Microsoft Account.

7 Click on your own entry to view your profile. If you have linked it to different accounts these will be displayed. Click on one of the accounts to edit the entries

← People

EDIT LINKED CONTACT

Name

Nick Vandome

Edit Outlook
Nick Vandome

Edit Outlook (?)
Nick Vandome

Edit iCloud

8 Edit and save the required details in the same way as for creating a new entry

← People

EDIT OUTLOOK CONTACT

Add photo

Name

Nick Vandome

+ Phone

Personal email ∨

nickvandome@googlemail.com

Chatting with Skype

Skype is one of the premier services for free voice calls (to other Skype users) and instant messaging for text messages. It can now be incorporated into your Windows 10 experience and used to keep in touch with family, friends and work colleagues at home and around the world.

 Skype can be downloaded for free from the Windows Store, if it is not already installed on your computer. Click on the **Install** button

Click on the Skype button on the Start Menu or in the **All Apps** section

If you already have a Skype account you can sign in with these details, or with your Microsoft account details. Click on **Create an account** to create a new Skype account

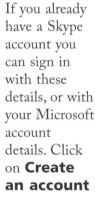 Once you have entered your Skype login details you can check your speakers, microphone and webcam, for voice and video calls. Click on the **Continue** button

5 Skype contacts are shown here. Tap on one to start a voice or video call or text message

6 Click in this box to start a text conversation

7 Click on the phone button to make a voice call or the video button to make a video call

8 Click in the search box to look for other Skype contacts. Click on the **Search Skype** button

Nick Vandome
Online

Q Alex Goodall

Search Skype

9 Click on this button next to someone in the search results to add them as a contact

Alex Goodall
United Kingdom

Don't forget

When you create a text conversation with one of your contacts in Skype, it will continue down the page as you respond to each other.

Don't forget

When you add someone as a contact you have to send them a contact request, which they must accept to become one of your contacts.

Beware

Do not accept requests from people you don't know. If you receive one of these, click on **Decline** when they send you a request.

Using the Calendar

The Calendar app can be used to record important events and reminders. To view the calendar:

1 Click on the **Calendar** app on the Start Menu, or access it from **All apps**

2 Click on the **Get started** button

Accounts can be added to the Calendar app in the same way as for the Mail and People apps.

3 Select an account to link with your calendar (or add a new one) and click on the **Ready to go** button

4 Click here to view specific months and click on the top toolbar to view by **Day**, **Work week**, **Week**, **Month** or **Today**

5 Click on these buttons to move between months (or swipe left or right on a touchpad)

206

Adding events

Events can be added to the calendar and various settings can be applied to them, such as recurrence and reminders.

 Click on a date to create a new event or click on the **New event** button

Reminders can be set for calendar events and these appear in the **Notifications** section. Click on this box on the top toolbar to set a time period for a reminder.

Reminder: 12 hours

 Enter details for the event in Step 1 or click on the **More details** button to access more fields

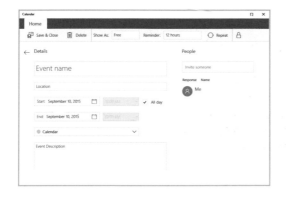

Click on the **Start** field and enter a time for the event

| Start: | September 10, 2015 | | 11:00 AM | ✓ | All day |
| End: | September 10, 2015 | | 1:00 PM | ✓ | |

If **All day** is selected, the time in the **Start** field will be grayed-out

...cont'd

5 For a recurring event, click on this button on the top toolbar

6 Select an option for the recurrence, such as **Weekly** and select a day for the recurrence

Repeat

Start: September 10, 2015

Weekly ⌄

Every | 1 ⌄ | week(s) on

☐ Su ☐ Mo ☐ Tu ☐ We

✓ Th ☐ Fr ☐ Sa

End: Never

Hot tip

If you have connected the People app to your other accounts, such as Facebook or Twitter, the birthdays of your contacts from these sites will automatically be added to your calendar.

7 Click on the **Save & Close** button in the main window to save the event

Save & Close

8 To delete an existing event, click on it and click on the **Edit occurrence** button

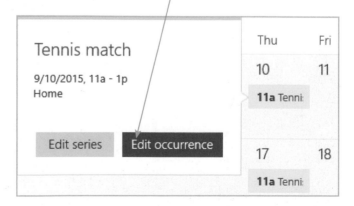

Tennis match

9/10/2015, 11a - 1p
Home

Edit series | Edit occurrence

	Thu	Fri
	10	11
	11a Tenni:	
	17	18
	11a Tenni:	

9 Click on the **Delete** button

🗑 Delete

11 Networking

Windows 10 has a built-in networking capability, allowing you to share a variety of items between two or more computers. This chapter shows how this can be done and how to set up the HomeGroup feature for file sharing.

210 Network Components

211 Set Up Your Network

212 Internet Connection

214 Discover Networks

215 Network and Sharing Center

216 Join the HomeGroup

217 Sharing Files and Folders

218 Sharing Settings

219 View Network Components

220 Network Troubleshooting

Network Components

There are numerous possibilities for setting up a home network. To start with, there are two major network technologies:

● **Wired** – e.g. Ethernet, using twisted pair cables, to send data at rates of 10, 100 or 1000 Mbps (megabits per second).

● **Wireless** – using radio waves to send data at rates of 11 or 54 Mbps (or up to, in theory, 300 Mbps with the latest devices).

There is also a variety of hardware items needed:

● **Network adapter** – appropriate to the network type, with one for each computer in the network.

● **Network controller** – one or more hub, switch or router, providing the actual connection to each network adapter.

There is also the internet connection (dial-up, DSL or cable) using:

● A modem connected to one of the computers

● A modem connected to the network

● Internet access incorporated into the router or switch

Don't forget

The network adapter can be connected to the USB port, inserted in the PC Card slot or installed inside your computer.

Don't forget

Ethernet adapters connect to a network hub, switch or wired router. Wireless adapters connect through a wireless router or a combination of router/switch.

Hot tip

You may already have some of these elements in operation, if you have an existing network running a previous version of Windows.

Set Up Your Network

The steps you will need, and the most appropriate sequence to follow, will depend on the specific options on your system. However, the main steps will include:

- Install network adapters in the computers, where necessary

- Set up or verify the internet connection

- Configure the wireless router or access point

- Connect other computers and start up Windows on each PC

Install Hardware

If you need to install a wired or wireless network adapter, follow the instructions provided with the adapter. For example, to install the Linksys Wireless-N USB adapter:

1 Insert the CD provided and the setup program will start up automatically. Select the **Click Here to Start** button

2 Follow the instructions (giving permission for access where requested) to complete the software installation

3 When prompted, attach the adapter to a USB port, via a cable if needed

4 When Windows has detected the wireless networks in your neighborhood, select your network and click on the **Connect** button

With all the options and combinations that might be available, configuring the network could be complex. However, Windows 10 is designed to automate as much of the task as possible.

Depending on the AutoPlay settings (**Settings > Devices > AutoPlay**), you may be prompted to run the installation option when you insert the CD.

Enter the security key for your wireless network when prompted.

Internet Connection

You do not actually require an internet connection to set up a network, if all you want to do is share files and printers. However, in most cases the main purpose of the network is to share your connection to the internet across several computers.

Verify your Connection

If you already have an internet connection, open your web browser and go to a website that gets regularly updated (e.g. a news site). If the website opens with up-to-date entries and you don't get an error message, your connection is working.

Install Router

You can use a router with a DSL modem (an internet gateway) to make an internet connection available for sharing. This is usually set up on one computer, connected via an Ethernet cable or a USB cable. A configuration program may be provided on an installation CD or you can use your web browser.

If your router has been installed, Windows will automatically complete the connection to the internet.

 Open the browser and enter the IP address provided for the router, e.g. 192.168.1.254 or a similar local IP address

If you go to a website that stays relatively static, some of its web pages might be stored on your computer and will display correctly even if your connection is faulty.

 Select **Settings** and enter the administrator username (if required) and password, as provided by your ISP

You will be using the default ID and password for the particular equipment. While this can only be accessed from a direct local connection, you may feel more secure if you change the password.

3 Select **Admin Password**, then enter the old password and the new password and click **Change password**

BT Home Hub manager - Admin Password - Windows Internet Explorer

http://192.168.1.254/password.lp?be=0&l0=2&l1=5&l2=-1

Google

Favorites   BT Home Hub manager - Admin Password

Page ▼

BT Home Hub   Help | A-Z

| Home | Services | Settings | Troubleshooting |

Wireless   Telephones   Internet
                    BT Power   BT Access   Application   Admin   Advanced
                    Save   Control   Sharing   Password   Settings

Admin Password

You'll be asked to enter this password before you can access the set-up options in your Hub Manager.

Your password is case sensitive and needs to be 5-20 characters long and without spaces. You can use letters, numbers and punctuation. Your new password shouldn't be anything that someone else can easily guess.

Old password: ••••••••••
Enter new password: ••••••••••
Confirm new password: ••••••••••   Advice for a secure password

Please keep a note of your new password. If you can't remember it, you'll need to reset your Hub to its default settings so you can then access your Hub Manager and choose another password.

                                                    Change password

Internet | Protected Mode: On   100%

The options offered will depend on the particular features of your router or gateway device, but they should, in principle, be similar.

4 Select **Wireless** to change the setup, for example by providing a new SSID (Service Set Identifier, the wireless network name) and choosing the encryption type and key

BT Home Hub manager - Wireless Set-up - Windows Internet Explorer

http://192.168.1.254/wireless.lp?be=0&l0=2&l1=0&l2=-1

Google

Favorites   BT Home Hub manager - Wireless Set-up

Page ▼

BT Home Hub   Help | A-Z

| Home | Services | Settings | Troubleshooting |

Wireless   Telephones   Internet
                    BT Power   BT Access   Application   Admin   Advanced
                    Save   Control   Sharing   Password   Settings

Wireless Set-up

Wireless network name (SSID)   BTHomeHub2-NR99
Encryption: ◯ Use WEP
                                ◉ Use WPA & WPA2
WPA-PSK Encryption Key: ••••••••••
                                Between 8 and 63 characters (which can be letters, numbers and
                                punctuation). Advice for a secure key

                                            Reset wireless security to default

Internet | Protected Mode: On   100%

Do not use the default values for the parameters since these could be known to other people.

5 You can also change the channels used for the wireless communications, if you have problems with network range or speed, or interference from other devices

Discover Networks

You can connect your computers to form a network, using Ethernet cables and adapters or by setting up your wireless adapters and routers. When you start up each computer, Windows 10 will examine the current configuration and discover any new networks that have been established since the last start up. You can check this, or connect manually to a network, from within the default settings from the Settings. To do this:

1 Click on the **Settings** app and click on the **Network & Internet** button

Network & Internet
Wi-Fi, airplane mode,
VPN

Beware

If your network is unavailable, for any reason, this will be noted in Step 2.

2 Drag the Wi-Fi button to **On**. Under the **Wi-Fi** heading, click on one of the available networks

3 Check on the **Connect automatically** box and click on the **Connect** button to connect to the selected network

4 The selected network is shown as **Connected**. This is also shown in the Notifications area

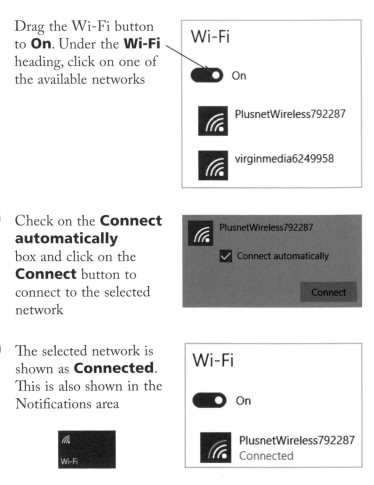

Network and Sharing Center

The Network and Sharing Center within the Control Panel is
where you can view settings for your network.

1 To open the Network and
Sharing Center, access the
Control Panel and click on
the **Network and Internet** link

> Network and Internet
> View network status and tasks
> Choose homegroup and sharing options

2 Click on the **Network
and Sharing Center**
link

> Network and Sharing Center
> View network status and tasks | Connect to a network
> View network computers and devices
>
> HomeGroup
> Choose homegroup and sharing options
>
> Internet Options
> Change your homepage | Manage browser add-ons
> Delete browsing history and cookies

3 Details of the current network are displayed in the
Network and Sharing Center

4 Click on the **Connections**
link to see details of your Wi-Fi
connection

> Access type: Internet
> HomeGroup: Ready to create
> Connections: Wi-Fi
>   (PlusnetWireless792287)

5 The Wi-Fi information
is displayed. Click on the
Properties button for more
information

Don't
forget

The Network and
Sharing Center displays
network settings and
provides access to
networking tasks on the
computer.

Hot tip

In the Network and
Sharing Center, click
on the **Set up a
new connection or
network** link to create
a different network from
the one currently in use.

Join the HomeGroup

A HomeGroup is a network function that enables a Windows 10 computer to connect to another Windows 10 machine (or Windows 7/8) and share content. You can set up and connect to the HomeGroup through the Control Panel:

Don't forget

When you add a computer to your network, Windows 10 on that computer will detect that there is a HomeGroup already created.

Beware

HomeGroup applies to any user with an account on the computer, so if a different user logs on, the associated files will also be accessible.

Don't forget

Windows generates the password when the HomeGroup is created. If you forget the password, you can find it in the Control Panel on any computer already joined to the HomeGroup.

1 Access **Network and Internet** in the Control Panel and click on the **HomeGroup** link

2 Click on the **Create a homegroup** button to start setting up the HomeGroup

3 Click on the **Next** button

4 Select the items that you want to share in the HomeGroup and click on the **Next** button

5 Enter the password that has to be provided from the other computer. Click on the **Finish** button. Once you have joined the HomeGroup you will be able to share your files on the other computer and vice versa

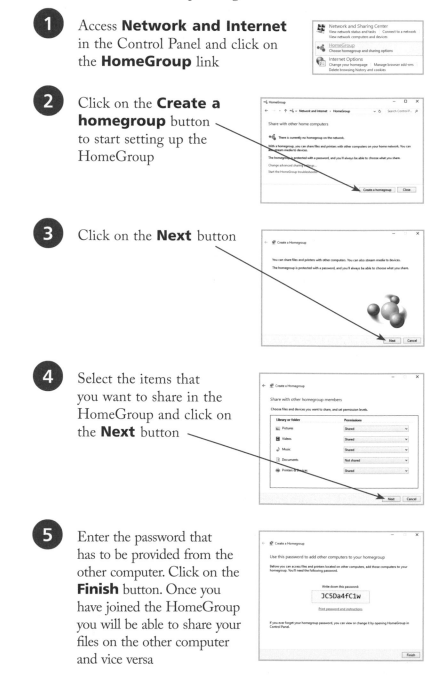

Sharing Files and Folders

There are different ways in which you can share items once a HomeGroup has been set up:

1 Open File Explorer and select the **HomeGroup** in the Library pane, then click on the **Share libraries** button in the Share section of the File Explorer

2 Select the items that you want to share with the HomeGroup. This will be done automatically, i.e. if you share Pictures then all of the items in the Pictures library will be shared, as will new ones that are added

Don't forget

The Share section in File Explorer is accessed from the Scenic Ribbon.

3 To share a specific item, select it in File Explorer and click on the **HomeGroup** button in the Share section

4 Select HomeGroup in the Navigation pane of the File Explorer Library pane to view the shared item in Step 3

Sharing Settings

Within the Network and Sharing Center there are also options for specifying how items are shared over the network, not just in the HomeGroup. To select these:

 Open the Network and Sharing Center and click on the **Change advanced sharing settings** link

Change advanced sharing settings

 Select sharing options for different networks, including private, guest or public and all networks. Options can be selected for turning on network discovery so that your computer can see other computers on the network, and file and printer sharing

Don't forget

If you are sharing over a network you should be able to access the Public folder on another computer (providing that network discovery is turned on). If you are the administrator of the other computer you will also be able to access your own Home folder, although you will need to enter the required password for this (see page 216).

Click on these arrows to view the options for each network category

View Network Components

You can also view the components of the network in File Explorer. To do this:

1 Open File Explorer and click on the **Network** link

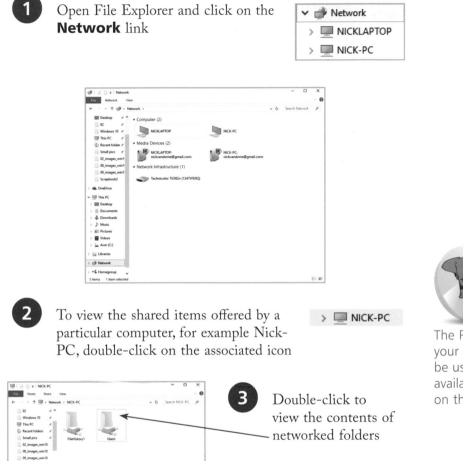

2 To view the shared items offered by a particular computer, for example Nick-PC, double-click on the associated icon

> 🖥 NICK-PC

3 Double-click to view the contents of networked folders

219

Don't forget

The Public folder on your own computer can be used to make items available to other users on the network.

Public files and folders plus those belonging to the currently-active user are available to access. Items can be copied here for sharing purposes.

Network Troubleshooting

Windows 10 provides several troubleshooters to resolve common problems with networks. They are downloaded, so you can always get the most up-to-date help.

1 Open the Network and Sharing Center and select **Troubleshoot problems**

Troubleshoot problems
Diagnose and repair network problems, or get troubleshooting information.

2 Windows searches online for troubleshooting packs

Network and Internet — □ ×

← → ∨ ↑ 🖳 « Troublesho... › Network and Internet   ∨ ⟳   Search Troublesh... 🔎

Troubleshoot problems - Network and Internet

Network ▲

Internet Connections
Find and fix problems with connecting to the Internet or to websites.

Shared Folders
Find and fix problems with accessing files and folders on other computers.

HomeGroup
Find and fix problems with viewing computers or shared files in a homegroup.

Network Adapter
Find and fix problems with wireless and other network adapters.

Incoming Connections
Find and fix problems with incoming computer connections and Windows Firewall.

Printing ▲

Printer
Find and fix problems with printing.

3 Select, for example, Shared Folders and follow the prompts to find and hopefully resolve the problems

In this case, a problem accessing a folder on another computer is quickly resolved as a typing error, when Windows says it cannot find "windows10" but detects the similar folder name "Windows 10" (with a space before 10).

×

← 🔲 Shared Folders

Troubleshoot and help prevent computer problems

Shared Folders
Find and fix problems with accessing files and folders on other computers.

Advanced

Publisher: Microsoft Corporation
Privacy statement

Next   Cancel

12 System and Security

Windows 10 includes tools to help maintain your hard drive, protect your computer from malicious software, back up your files, folders and apps and keep your system up-to-date.

222 System Properties

224 Clean Up Your Disk

226 Windows Update

227 Back Up and Recover Data

228 System Restore

230 Security and Maintenance

231 Windows Firewall

232 Malware Protection

System Properties

There are several ways to open the System Properties, and view information about your computer:

1 Access the **Control Panel, System and Security** and then click on the **System** category

2 Press the **WinKey** + the **Pause/Break** keys

3 Right-click **This PC** in the File Explorer and select **Properties** from the menu

4 Right-click on the **Start** button and select **System** from the contextual menu

The main panel provides the Windows 10 edition, processor details, memory size, computer and network names, and Windows 10 activation status. There are also links to the Device Manager and to more advanced settings.

...cont'd

Device Manager

1 Select **Device Manager**, to list all of the hardware components that are installed on your computer

2 Select the › symbol to expand that entry to show details

3 Select the ⌄ symbol to collapse the expanded entry

4 Double-click any device to open its properties

5 Select the Driver tab and select **Update Driver** to find and install new software

6 Select **Disable** to put the particular device offline. The button changes to **Enable**, to reverse the action

You may be prompted for an administrator password or asked for permission to continue, when you select some Device Manager entries.

Click on the **Roll Back Driver** button to switch back to the previously-installed driver for that device, if the new one fails.

223

Clean Up Your Disk

1. In File Explorer, right-click **OS (C:)** and click on the **Properties** link

> 🎬 Videos
> 💾 Acer (C:)   **Properties**

2. Click on the **Disk Cleanup** button

■ Used space:	116,160,184,320 bytes	108 GB
■ Free space:	612,729,106,432 bytes	570 GB
Capacity:	728,889,290,752 bytes	678 GB

Drive C: Disk Cleanup

3. Disk Cleanup scans the drive to identify files that can be safely removed

Disk Cleanup   ✕
Disk Cleanup is calculating how much space you will be able to free on Acer (C:). This may take a few minutes to complete.
Calculating...   Cancel
Scanning: System error memory dump files

Don't forget

You can have more than one hard disk on your computer.

4. All of the possible files are listed by category, and the sets of files recommended to be deleted are marked with a tick symbol

Disk Cleanup for Acer (C:)   ✕

Disk Cleanup

You can use Disk Cleanup to free up to 66.5 MB of disk space on Acer (C:).

Files to delete:
- ☑ Downloaded Program Files   0 bytes
- ☑ Temporary Internet Files   32.0 MB
- ☐ Delivery Optimization Files   0 bytes
- ☐ Recycle Bin   6.39 MB
- ☐ Temporary files   0 bytes

Total amount of disk space you gain: 60.1 MB

Description
Downloaded Program Files are ActiveX controls and Java applets downloaded automatically from the Internet when you view certain pages. They are temporarily stored in the Downloaded Program Files folder on your hard disk.

[Clean up system files]   [View Files]
How does Disk Cleanup work?
      [OK]   [Cancel]

5. Make changes to the selections, clicking **View Files** if necessary to help you choose

6. Select the button **Clean up system files**, to include also these, then select **OK**

7. Deleted files will not be transferred to the Recycle Bin, so confirm that you do want to permanently delete all of these files. The files will be removed and the disk space will become available

Disk Cleanup   ✕
Are you sure you want to permanently delete these files?
      [Delete Files]   [Cancel]

Disk Cleanup   ✕
The Disk Cleanup utility is cleaning up unnecessary files on your machine.
Cleaning up drive Acer (C:).
      [Cancel]
Cleaning: Device driver packages

When a file is written to the hard disk, it may be stored in several pieces in different places. This fragmentation of disk space can slow down your computer. Disk Defragmenter rearranges the data so the disk will work more efficiently.

1 In the File Explorer, right-click on **OS (C:)** and click on the **Properties** link

2 Select the **Tools** tab and click on the **Optimize** button

Don't forget

The spellings are localized.

3 The process runs as a scheduled task, but you can select a drive and select **Analyze** to check out a new drive

Hot tip

Only disks that can be fragmented are shown. These can include USB drives that you add to your system.

4 Click the **Optimize** button to process the selected disk. This may take between several minutes to several hours to complete, depending on the size and state of the disk, but you can still use your computer while the task is running

Windows Update

Updates to Windows 10 and other Microsoft products are supplied regularly, to help prevent or fix problems, improve the security or enhance performance. The way in which they are downloaded and installed can be specified from the Settings app:

1 Access the **Settings** app and click on the **Update & security** button

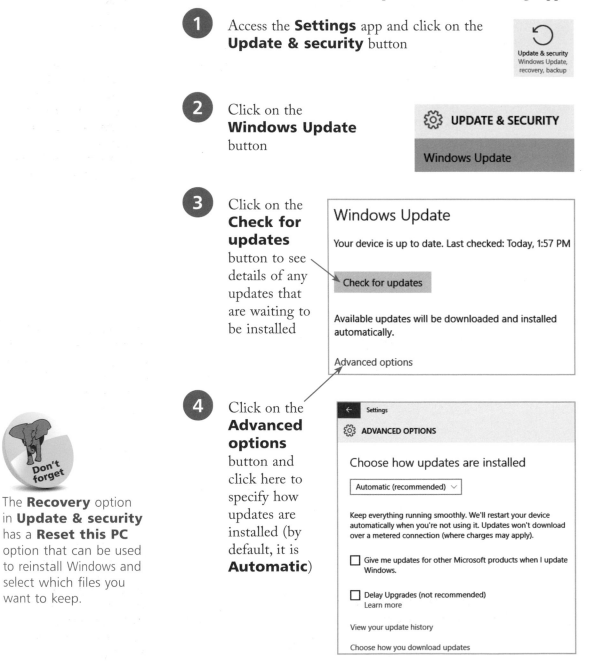

↺

Update & security
Windows Update,
recovery, backup

2 Click on the **Windows Update** button

⚙ UPDATE & SECURITY

Windows Update

3 Click on the **Check for updates** button to see details of any updates that are waiting to be installed

Windows Update

Your device is up to date. Last checked: Today, 1:57 PM

Check for updates

Available updates will be downloaded and installed automatically.

Advanced options

4 Click on the **Advanced options** button and click here to specify how updates are installed (by default, it is **Automatic**)

← Settings

⚙ ADVANCED OPTIONS

Choose how updates are installed

Automatic (recommended) ∨

Keep everything running smoothly. We'll restart your device automatically when you're not using it. Updates won't download over a metered connection (where charges may apply).

☐ Give me updates for other Microsoft products when I update Windows.

☐ Delay Upgrades (not recommended)
   Learn more

View your update history

Choose how you download updates

Don't forget

The **Recovery** option in **Update & security** has a **Reset this PC** option that can be used to reinstall Windows and select which files you want to keep.

Back Up and Recover Data

1 Open the **Control Panel** and select **Save backup copies of your files with File History**, in the **System and Security** category

2 The first time you do this, you can select a drive such as an external hard drive or a network drive. Click on the **Turn on** button to back up copies of your files

3 Details of the backup are displayed here

Keep a history of your files

File History saves copies of your files so you can get them back if they're lost or damaged.

File History is on

Copy files from: Libraries, Desktop, Contacts, and Favorites
Copy files to:

Seagate Slim Drive (E:)
6.21 GB free of 465 GB

File History is saving copies of your files for the first time.
Stop

Turn off

4 Click on the **Run now** link to perform another backup

Seagate Slim Drive (E:)
6.21 GB free of 465 GB
Run now

You can also back up files through the Settings app. To do this, select **Settings > Update & Security > Backup** and drag the **Automatically back up my files** button to **On**.

You can create a system image (an exact copy of a drive) and also back up data files in the libraries and other folders on your system.

Items that have been backed up can be recovered through the Control Panel by selecting **System and Security > Backup and Restore > Restore files from backup**.

System Restore

Windows 10 takes snapshots of the system files before any software updates are applied, or in any event once every seven days. You can also create a snapshot manually. The snapshots are known as Restore Points and are managed by System Restore.

1 From the Control Panel, open **System** under **System and Security** and select **System protection**

System Restore returns system files to an earlier point in time, allowing you to undo system changes without affecting your documents, email, and other data files.

228

2 Select the **Create** button, to create a restore point manually

3 Provide a title for the restore point and click **Create**

4 The required data is written to disk and the manual restore point is set up

System Restore is not intended for protecting personal data files. For these you should use Windows Backup (see previous page).

Using Restore Points

The installation of a new app or driver software may make Windows 10 behave unpredictably or have other unexpected results. Usually, uninstalling the app or rolling back the driver (see page 223) will correct the situation. If this does not fix the problem, use an automatic or manual restore point to reset your system to an earlier date when everything worked correctly.

1 Select **System Protection** and click the **System Restore** button

System Restore...

2 By default this will offer to undo the most recent change. This may fix the problem

You can also run System Restore from Safe Mode, the troubleshooting option. Start up the computer and press **F8** repeatedly as your computer reboots, to display the boot menu, then select **Safe Mode**.

System Restore

Restore system files and settings

System Restore can help fix problems that might be making your computer run slowly or stop responding.

System Restore does not affect any of your documents, pictures, or other personal data. Recently installed programs and drivers might be uninstalled.

● Recommended restore:

Select this option to undo the most recent update, driver, or software installation if you think it is causing problems.

Time: 5/28/2015 11:14:04 AM
Description: Install: Windows Modules Installer
Current time zone: GMT Daylight Time

Scan for affected programs

○ Choose a different restore point

< Back   Next >   Cancel

3 Otherwise, click **Choose a different restore point**, and pick a suitable time

If the selected restore point does not resolve the problem, you can try again, selecting another restore point.

System Restore

Restore your computer to the state it was in before the selected event

Current time zone: GMT Daylight Time

Date and Time	Description	Type
5/28/2015 2:45:09 PM	Pre Windows 10	Manual
5/28/2015 11:14:04 AM	Windows Modules Installer	Install
5/26/2015 3:19:54 PM	Windows Update	Critical Update

Scan for affected programs

< Back   Next >   Cancel

4 Follow the prompts to restart the system using system files from the selected date and time

Security and Maintenance

The Security and Maintenance section in the Control Panel monitors security and delivers alerts for security features.

1 In the Control Panel, click on the **Security and Maintenance** link in **System and Security**

Security and Maintenance
Review your computer's status and resolve issues
Change User Account Control settings
Troubleshoot common computer problems

2 Click on the icon for more details, then select the **Change Security and Maintenance settings** link

Hot tip

In the Security and Maintenance settings you can also change User Account Control settings.

3 Check the settings On or Off as required

Windows Firewall

1 Open Control Panel, select the System and Security category and select **Windows Firewall**

Windows Firewall
Check firewall status
Allow an app through Windows Firewall

2 Select **Turn Windows Firewall on or off** to customize settings for private (home and work) and public networks

3 Select **Allow an app or feature through Windows Firewall**, to view the allowed apps

Allow an app or feature through Windows Firewall

4 Click on the **Change settings** button to allow or restrict apps

 Change settings

5 Check apps On or Off to allow them or remove them from the allowed list. Click on the **OK** button to apply the changes

Hot tip

The Windows Firewall can be used to provide a level of protection against malicious software and viruses.

Don't forget

Firewall is on by default in Windows 10, but you can turn it off if you have another Firewall installed and active.

Beware

Only add apps to the allowed list if you are advised to do so by a trusted advisor, or if you trust their origins.

Malware Protection

The Windows Defender app, that is pre-installed with Windows 10, can be used to give a certain amount of protection against virus and malicious software. To use it:

1 Click here on the Taskbar, click on the Windows Defender icon and click **Open**

Malware (malicious software) is designed to deliberately harm your computer. To protect your system, you need up-to-date antivirus and anti-spyware software. Windows Defender provides the latter, but you should install a separate antivirus app.

2 For an immediate check, select the **Home** tab and click on the **Scan now** button

3 From the **Settings** app, select **Update & Security > Windows Defender** and adjust settings such as real-time protection and cloud-based protection

The default scan time is 2 am. If the computer is normally switched off before then, you will never get a scan. Make sure to choose a practical schedule time.

Index

Symbols

32-bit	20
64-bit	20

A

Access Action Center	
With swipe gesture	15
Access administration tools	
With keyboard shortcut	14
Access an app's toolbar	
With swipe gesture	15
Access Cortana	
With keyboard shortcut	14
With touchpad	15
Access File Explorer	
With keyboard shortcut	14
Access Quick access	
With keyboard shortcut	14
Access the Control Panel	
With keyboard shortcut	14
Access the Desktop	
With keyboard shortcut	14
Access the Ease of Access Center	
With keyboard shortcut	14
Access the Settings app	
With keyboard shortcut	14
Access the Sharing options	
With keyboard shortcut	14
Access the Start Menu	
With keyboard shortcut	14
Access the Task Manager	
With keyboard shortcut	14
Access the Task View	
With swipe gesture	15
Action Center.	See Notifications panel
Adding users.	See Users: Adding
Address bar	94, 128-129
Address book.	See People
Add to compressed folder	155
Adjacent block	138
All apps	
Grid	76
Viewing	76
All files and folders	139
Alternative programs	145

Apps.	See also Windows 10 apps
About	68-69
Buying	83
Classic	74
Closing	73, 75
Cost	83
Installing	86
Maximizing	73
Menus	73
Minimizing	73
Moving	72
Pin to Start screen	78
Pin to Taskbar	79
Reinstalling	84
Restrictions	65
Searching for	77
Switching	
Accessing with touch	15
Uninstalling	87
Using	72-73
Windows 10 apps	68
Windows classic apps	68
Windows Store	80-84
Windows Store apps	68
Apps view.	See All apps
Arrange icons	105
Arrange windows	98
Associated programs	145

B

Back button	94
Background	
Setting	40
Backtrack file operations	152
Back up	227
Bing	71
Broadband connection	180
Burn to disc	143
Bypass the Recycle Bin	149

C

Cable connection	180
Calculator	92

Calendar	206-208
Adding events	207-208
Cascade windows	98
Changing views	132
Character Map	158
Charms Bar	
Removal	12
Check box	93
Classic themes	41
Clean Install	13
Clean up your disk	224-225
Close an app	
With keyboard shortcut	14
Close window	96, 106
Collapse	127
Command button	93
Compare windows	101
Compressed folders	155
Compressed item properties	156
Conflicts with files and folders	144
Connect new devices	
With keyboard shortcut	14
Connect to the Internet	181
Contacts.	See People
Continuum	15
Control icon	94-95
Control menu	95, 106
Control menu move	95
Control menu size	97
Control Panel	222
Accessing	23
Copy a character	158
Copy files and folders	140
Cortana	58-61
Notebook	61
Searching with	60
Settings	61
Setting up	58
Setting up the microphone	59
Using	59-61
Create compressed folder	155
Create folders	150
Cut, Copy, Paste files and folders	142

D

Date and time functions	116
Deactivate Recycle Bin	149
Delete files and folders	146
Depth of field	173
Desktop	32, 129
Accessing	23
Accessing with shortcuts	32
From the keyboard	14
Desktop icons	105, 111
Desktops	
Adding	36-37
Deleting	37
Details view	133
Device Manager	223
Dialog box	93
Dial-up connection	180
Digital Subscriber Line (DSL)	180
Dimmed option	92
Discover networks	214
Disk defragmenter	225
Display menu bar	92
Display settings	113, 119
Display the Lock screen	
With keyboard shortcut	14
Display the thumbnails on the Taskbar	
With keyboard shortcut	14
Documents	128, 154
Drag files and folders	141
DVDs	
Issue with playing	177

E

Ease of Access	
From login screen	18
Ease of Access Center	114-115
From the keyboard	14
Magnifier	115
Recommendations	114
Ethernet	210
Explorer.	See File Explorer
Exploring drives	126
Extract files and folders	156

F

Facebook	208
Family Safety	65
File Explorer	
Close	134
From the keyboard	14
Open	118
View	130
File properties	153

Files and folders
    Burn to Disc   143
    Conflicts   144
    Copy   140
    Create   150
    Cut, Copy, Paste   142
    Delete   146
    Drag   141
    Move   140
    Rename   151
    Search   154
    Select   138-139
File type   150
Filtering   134
Find a character   158
Firewall.   *See* Windows Firewall
Folder options   93, 136
Font samples   157
Fonts folder   157
Forward   94
Frequently used apps
    On the Start Menu   24
Full screen mode   26

G

Games
    Playing   178
Gestures   15
GMail   196
Graphical User Interface (GUI)   8
Grayed option   92
Groove Music app   174
Group by   105, 135
Grouping   135
Groups
    On the Start Menu   28
        Editing names   29
        Naming   29
Group task buttons   119
Guest Account   64

H

Hard disk drive   123
Hide file extensions   150
Hide menu bar   92
HomeGroup   127
    Join   216

Hotmail
    Renamed   196

I

Insert a character   158
Install app   86
Install router   212
Internet connection   180, 212
Internet Explorer   182
Internet Service Provider (ISP)   180

J

Jump List   26

K

Keyboard shortcuts   14

L

Libraries   120-121, 127, 133
    Properties   153
Library
    File menu   121
    Home menu   121
    Manage menu   122
    Menu options   122
    Share menu   122
    View menu   122
Library location   120
Library tools   121
Live preview   104, 119
Live Tile functionality   85
    Calendar   85
    Groove Music   85
    Mail   85
    Money   85
    News   85
    People   85
    Photos   85
    Sport   85

Live Tiles	85
Local account	
Signing in with	19
Location	123
Locking the screen	
From the keyboard	14
Locking your computer	18
Lock screen	18
Notifications	43
Settings	42-43
Logging in	See Signing in
Login settings	See Sign-in settings

M

Magnifier	115
Mail	196-201
Accounts	196
Formatting	199
POP3 account	196
Sending	198-199
Setting up	196-197
Malware protection	232
Maximize	94, 95
Media Player.	See Windows Media Player
Menu bar	92
Microsoft Account	16-17
Creating	16-17
Email address	64
Prompted to create	16
Services	16
Microsoft Edge	
About	182
Accessing favorites	190
Adding Notes	187-188
Bookmarking pages	186
Browsing history	191
Clear history	191
Downloads	191
Find on page	194
Hub	190-191
Importing favorites	184
InPrivate browsing	194
Menu Options	194
Open with Internet Explorer	194
Print	194
Reading List	190, 192
Reading View	193
Setting a Homepage	184
Settings	194
Sharing clippings	189

Sharing notes	189
Smart address bar	183
Tabs	185
Zoom	194
Microsoft Windows.	See Windows
Minimize	94
Mouse pointer	94
Move files and folders	140
Move window	95
Movies and TV	
Viewing	177
MS-DOS	8
Multimonitor support	95
Multiple windows	102-103
Music	
Playing	175
Playing your own	175-176

N

Navigation panes	123, 130-131
Details pane	131
Preview pane	131
Netflix	178
Network	127
Components	210
Discover networks	214
Install hardware	211
Install router	212
Internet connection	212
Setup	211
Troubleshooting	220
View components	219
Network and Sharing Center	215
Troubleshooting	220
Networked drive	123
Non-adjacent files	139
Notepad	92
Notifications	12, 38-39
On the Lock screen	43
Settings	39
Notifications panel	
On the Taskbar	32

O

OneDrive	
Adding files	164-165
Online	162

Settings   163
Sharing   165
Using   160
Open files   145
Open window   98, 106
Optimizing folders   122
Outlook   196

P

Peek   99
People   200-203
   Adding contacts manually   202-203
   Finding   200-203
Permanently erase files   148
Personalization
   Look and feel   40-41
Personalize Windows   119
   Desktop icons   111
   Screen Saver   110
Photos
   App   166-173
   Editing   170-171
      Undo   173
   Importing   166
   Viewing   166-169
Picture password   19
PIN   19
Pin to Start Menu   78
Pin to Taskbar   79
Power button   12
Power off button   18
Power Options   22
Precision touchpads   15
Pre-install   13
Preserve file types   151
Preview window   104
Printers
   Adding   47

Q

Quick access folder
   File location   124
   In File Explorer   124-125
   Pinning items   125
Quick access settings
   On the Notifications panel   12

R

Radio button   93
Recover data   227
Recycle Bin   147, 224
   Bypass   149
   Deactivate   149
   Empty   148
   Permanently erase files   148
   Resize   149
   Restoring files   147
Redo   152
Reminders   62-63
   Completed   63
Removing users.   See Users: Removing
Rename files and folders   151
Resize window   97
Resource Monitor   90
Restart   33
   For updates   33
Restore point   228
Restore window   94, 96, 101
Reveal file extensions   150
Ribbon.   See Scenic Ribbon
Ruler   94
Run function   86

S

Safe Mode   229
Save your work   106
Scenic Ribbon   92, 94, 121-122
Screen resolution   112
Screen Saver   110
Scroll bars   94
Search
   Character map   158
   Files and folders   154
Search box   12, 94, 123
Searching   56-57
   Asking a question   57
   Over your computer   57
   Text search   56
   The web   57
Security and Maintenance   230
Select files and folders   138
Service Set Identifier (SSI)   213
Settings   44-55
   Accessing   44
   Account   50

237

Family & other users	50
Sign-in options	50
Sync your settings	50
Work access	50
Your account	50
Adding to the Taskbar	44
Devices	47
AutoPlay	47
Bluetooth	47
Connected devices	47
Mouse & touchpad	47
Printers & scanners	47
Typing	47
Ease of Access	52
Closed captions	52
High contrast	52
Keyboard	52
Magnifier	52
Mouse	52
Narrator	52
Other options	52
Network & Internet	48
Airplane mode	48
Data usage	48
Dial-up	48
Ethernet	48
Proxy	48
VPN	48
Wi-Fi	48
Personalization	49
Background	49
Colors	49
Lock screen	49
Start	49
Themes	49
Privacy	53
Account info	53
Background apps	53
Calendar	53
Camera	53
Contacts	53
Feedback & diagnostics.	53
General	53
Location	53
Messaging	53
Microphone	53
Other devices	53
Radios	53
Speech, inking & typing	53
System	45-46
About	46
Apps & features	45
Battery saver	46
Default apps	46

Display	45
Multitasking	45
Notifications & actions	45
Offline maps	46
Power & sleep	46
Storage	46
Tablet mode	45
Time & language	51
Date & time	51
Region & language	51
Speech	51
Update & security	54
Activation	55
Backup	55
For developers	55
Recovery	55
Windows Defender	55
Windows Update	54
Sharing	12
Shortcut keys	92, 100, 106, 142
Shortcuts	
For keyboard	14
Show Desktop	99
Show Desktop icons	99, 111
Shutting down	33
Affecting other users	66
From the Start button	33
Side-by-side windows	102-103
Sign-in options	18-19
Sign-in settings	19
Signing in	18-19
Skype	204-205
Contacts	205
Making calls	205
Sleep	33
Snaps	100
Snapshots with System Restore	228
Sort By option	135
Sorting files	133
Sound	109
Specifications	
For running Windows 10	10
Spin box	93
Stack windows	98
Start Button	22-23
Functionality	23
In previous versions	69
Shutting down from	33
Using	22
Start Menu	11, 24-25
All apps button	25
Back button	25
Customizing	26-27
Frequently used apps	24
Full screen mode	26

Power button 24
Removing items 27
Resizing tiles 30-31
Shutting down from 33
Transparency 49
Working with groups 28-29
Structure of the Desktop 32
Structure of window 94
Surface 3 tablet 11
Swiping gestures
For touch devices 15
Switch users 66
Switch windows 104
System properties 222
Device Manager 223
System Restore 228-229
For creating Restore Points 228

T

Tablets 11, 26
Tabs 93
Using in Microsoft Edge 185
Taskbar 32, 99, 119
From the keyboard 14
Notifications area 32
Pinning items 79
Transparency 49
Viewing open windows 32
Task button 96
Task Manager
From the keyboard 14
Performance 89
Processes 88
Task View 34-35
For viewing open apps 34
Task View button
Showing or hiding 34
Text Document file 150
Themes 41, 108
This PC
Folders 127
For accessing Properties 222
This PC folder 123
Tile windows 98
Tiles
Resizing 30-31
Time and date functions 116
Time controls 65
Title bar 94
Touch for Windows 10 15
Touchscreen devices 11, 15

Transparency 95
Troubleshooting 220
Turning off 33
Twitter 208

U

Undo 98, 152
Uninstall a program
From the Control Panel 45
Uninstalling apps 87
Unpinning apps 78-79
Updates
Restarting 33
Upgrading
From Windows 7 or 8 9
From Windows Vista 13
From Windows XP 13
To Windows 10 13
USB device 123, 126
User Accounts 64
Users
Adding 64-65
Removing 65
Using restore points 228

V

Videos
Library 177
Viewing 177
View available fonts 157
Viewing open apps 34-35
View network components 219
Voice calls
With Skype 204
Voice search
With Cortana 58-61

W

Web browser. *See* Microsoft Edge
Web filtering 65
Web searches 57
Windows 8
Editions 9-11

239

History   8
  Previous versions   8-9
Windows 7
  Upgrading from   9, 13
Windows 8   9
  Upgrading from   13
Windows 10   9
  About   9
  For touch   15
  Get Windows 10 app   13
  Installing   13
  Obtaining   13
Windows 10 apps   68, 70-71
  Alarms & Clock   70
  Calculator   70
  Calendar   70
  Camera   70
  Closing from the keyboard   14
  Food & Drink   70
  Fresh Paint   70
  Groove Music   70
  Health & Fitness   70
  Mail   70
  Maps   70
  Microsoft Edge   70
  Money   70
  Movies & TV   70
  News   70
  OneDrive   71
  OneNote   71
  People   71
  Photos   71
  Reader   71
  Reading List   71
  Settings   71
  Sport   71
  Store   71
  Toolbars
    Accessing with touch   15
  Weather   71
  Xbox   71
Windows 10 free upgrade
  Versions excluded   13
Windows 10 interface   10-11
Windows apps   68-69
Windows Firewall   231
Windows Hello   19
Windows Live Search.   See Bing
Windows logo key   66
Windows Media Player   177
Windows Phones   15
Windows Store
  About   80-82
  Buying apps   83
  Categories   82

Downloads   84
Featured apps   80
Home   82
Purchased apps   84
Ratings and reviews   81
Reinstalling apps   84
Updates to apps   84
Viewing your apps   84
Windows Store apps   69
Windows structure   94
Windows Update   226
Windows updates
  Restarting   33
Windows Vista
  Upgrading from   13
Windows XP
  Upgrading from   13
WinKey shortcuts   14
Winzip   155
Wireless   213
Wireless network   181, 210
WordPad   92, 94
Wrong password
  When signing in   18

X

Xbox 360   178
XP   8

Y

YouTube   178

Z

Zoom
  With Microsoft Edge   194